NAPOLEON

napoleon hill's

success masters

INTRODUCTION AND BONUS CONTENT BY
THE STAFF OF ENTREPRENEUR MEDIA, INC.

Entrepreneur Press®

Entrepreneur Press, Publisher
Cover Design: Andrew Welyczko
Production and Composition: Eliot House Productions

This publication is designed to provide accurate and authoritative information in regard
to the subject matter covered. It is sold with the understanding that the publisher is not
engaged in rendering legal, accounting, or other professional services. If legal advice or
other expert assistance is required, the services of a competent professional person should
be sought.

Entrepreneur Press® is a registered trademark of Entrepreneur Media, Inc.

Library of Congress Cataloging-in-Publication Data
Library of Congress Control Number: 2019944324
LC record available at https://lccn.loc.gov/2019944324

ISBN-13: 978-1-59918-649-8

Printed in the United States of America

23 22 21 20 19   10 9 8 7 6 5 4 3 2 1

Contents

CHAPTER NINE

Action Plan for Success: Your Psychological Needs

CHAPTER TEN

How to Get Control of Your Time and Your Life

CHAPTER ELEVEN

Power Over Problems

Foreword

Don M. Green, Executive Director
of Napoleon Hill Foundation

When W. Clement Stone, former chair of the Napoleon Hill Foundation, was given a copy of *Think and Grow Rich*, he was surprised that the principles listed in that book aligned with what he was already doing.

Mr. Stone was raised by his mother and learned two of Napoleon Hill's principles at an early age. His mother was a seamstress and W. Clement worked on the streets of Chicago to earn money as a newspaper boy. At the age of six, he was much smaller than most of the other newspaper boys and was often bullied for selling newspapers on what the other boys referred to as "their corner."

One day, W. Clement went into a restaurant and after selling a few newspapers was escorted to the door by the restaurant owner. Shortly thereafter, he returned to the same restaurant and began selling newspapers again. However, the owner forced him to leave for the second time. He returned to the restaurant for the third time, and the customers thought the ordeal was unacceptable, so they asked the restaurant owner to leave him alone.

His persistence, though, stood out. It is easy to see that Mr. Stone began practicing persistence at an early age. Apple founder Steve Jobs said that persistence was the most valuable trait he possessed.

W. Clement Stone's mother also taught him the importance of faith. No matter how tough the day had been, W. Clement and his mother always knelt at the foot of their beds and gave thanks. Practicing his faith helped him immensely as founder of Combined Insurance, a large and successful insurance broker, today known as Aon.

Even though Mr. Stone read *Think and Grow Rich* at a later age, he had already applied all the success principles to his insurance business. Starting with only $100, he built a fortune so large that he gave away hundreds of millions of dollars prior to his death at age 100.

In 1952, W. Clement Stone met the 69-year-old Napoleon Hill at a dental convention. At Mr. Stone's insistence, they formed an alliance and worked together for ten years, spreading the success principles that Napoleon Hill is known for the world over.

W. Clement Stone invested $500,000 to publish books with Napoleon Hill. Together, they wrote *Success through a Positive Mental Attitude* in 1960, which continues to sell well today.

Hill and Stone completed numerous speaking engagements and seminars all across the country. Many times, Mr. Stone would hold private conventions for his employees and hire well-known motivational speakers. He would record their lectures and furnish them to his employees for encouragement. This book is a composition of advice from some of these well-known speakers, enhanced by content and context for today's entrepreneur from the editors at *Entrepreneur Media*. Together, these two powerhouse brands showcase some of the best-known tenets of what it means to truly master success.

Introduction

By the Editors of Entrepreneur Media Inc.

Success is a shapeshifter. It looks different on each of us. What might exemplify success for one person may be anathema to another. One person's success may be wrapped in the temporal realm of money, power, or even fame. Another person's success may be defined by how they spend their time, or the connection between their work and passion. Yet another's may be defined in terms of what they don't have, as much as what they do.

No matter how you define it, we all seek success in one form or another. And the journey to find it can be long and often daunting. We hope for quick solutions; we don't often find them. We set our goals; often, too high. We depend on others to lay a path toward success for us, but it's not on them to do so. Ultimately, we find that the true key to success lies within.

Napoleon Hill knew this. He knew that success was entirely dependent on one element: you. And what YOU bring to the table is all you need to master the art of success, however you choose to define it.

Many well-known and trusted writers and speakers in the personal growth universe also knew that success is entirely dependent on the person who seeks it. That's why they have been chosen by The Napoleon Hill Foundation as "Masters of Success." In this book, personal development visionaries like W. Clement Stone, Earl Nightingale, and Dr. Norman Vincent Peale share their time-honored insights into success: how you can define it, how you can achieve it, and how you can hold onto it. Though each author approaches success differently, they all agree that the key to mastering success is inside each of us.

HOW TO USE THIS BOOK

The selections in this book from some of Napoleon Hill's timeless visionaries run the gamut from inspirational to practical. As you read, keep in mind that each essay is a product of its time and place. As such, some language usage and sentence construction may seem unfamiliar to you. We have opted to retain as much of the original tone and voice of the authors as possible, providing some updates for modern sensibilities, including headings to help you navigate the content. Our editors have also included some brief editorial comments as needed, which are noted in brackets.

Each selection includes a brief introduction, tips for the reader from our editors, and an "Entrepreneur Action Item" section to help you apply the lesson from each visionary to your own life and experience in a practical, actionable way. At the end of the book, you'll find a brief reader's guide packed with thought-provoking questions you can use in your reading group, class, or even for yourself to keep the conversation on success going.

HARNESS THE POWER OF YOUR IMAGINATION

Hill famously said, "All the breaks you need in life wait within your imagination . . . Imagination is the workshop of your mind, capable of turning mind energy into accomplishments and wealth." So what are you waiting for? Use your imagination to broaden your own idea of success. Think about what YOU want your life to look like. Do you want to grow in your position at work as an intrapreneur? Perhaps you want to forge a path outside the confines of your office and break out on your own as an entrepreneur. Maybe you want to create passive income that will allow you to focus more on goals. Or perhaps you want to focus on nonwork-related success: quality time with your family, honoring your interests and passions, or even having more time to volunteer and change your corner of the world. Success can look any way you want it to—all it takes is your imagination and the drive to make it happen. Let's get started!

CHAPTER ONE

Developing the Habits of a Winner

Dr. Denis Waitley

D r. Denis Waitley entered the Napoleon Hill universe when he was hired by W. Clement Stone, founder of Combined Insurance, to speak to 7,000 salespeople at the company. Dr. Waitley went on to produce recorded lectures that have been listened to by millions, and he became one of the world's premiere motivational speakers and writers. Some of his most well-known works include the essay "Developing Winner's Habits" and his bestselling audio, "The Psychology of Winning."

Waitley graduated from Annapolis and was a pilot with the Blue Angels, the Navy's precision flying team. He was a psychologist for the Apollo moon program and was a rehabilitating coordinator for America's returning Vietnam prisoners of war. He is also a member of the International Speakers Hall of Fame and developed the following ten attitudes and actions to help people become total winners:

- Positive Self-Awareness

- Positive Self-Esteem

- Positive Self-Control

- Positive Self-Motivation

- Positive Self-Expectancy

- Positive Self-Image

- Positive Self-Direction

- Positive Self-Dimension

- Positive Self-Discipline

- Positive Self-Projection

In this landmark essay, Waitley uses anecdotes from his own life to drive home some of the classic habits of winning that can elevate your level of success, including self-awareness and self-esteem.

❀ ❀ ❀

SELF-AWARENESS

I teach a program called POW, which everyone thinks means Prisoner of War. But I did it in Cambridge, England, and the little boys applauded when I put it up on the wall. They thought I meant the Prince of Wales. Later, I was in New York and Gloria Steinem saw me put POW up on the board, and she thought it meant Power of Woman! But in reality, the meaning of POW is Psychology of Winning. It always has been.

My father was right. He spent two years with me, age 7 to 9, and then he left home, but it didn't make any difference because my personality had already been formed. My dad came in and gave me the precious gift that too few parents today give. A new Harvard study shows we spend less than 60 seconds a day alone, one-on-one, with each child when they're most receptive to input, just before they go to bed. Less than 60 seconds a day alone with each child. Well, I spend time at the dinner table, and I spend time around the television set, and I tuck them in. My dad gave me more: 15 minutes a night, for two years. That was enough. He sat on my bed and told me the greatest thing I've ever heard. He said, "You know, I love you." And he also said, "By the way, you're born of special stuff, that's all. Your mother and I played Russian Roulette, and your chamber came up with the best of both of us. I don't know how you did it." He said, "Maybe it's our ancestry." He said, "I missed my ship. You'll catch yours." He said, "By the way, when I turn out the light for you, my son, it goes out all over the world. You see, light is to the eyes of the beholder, to the eyes of the receiver. It doesn't make any difference what's going on. It's how you take it. Keep your eyes open. Keep them shiny. Go for it. Don't worry about what I did. You don't have to be like me. You can choose to be different." Well, he's the greatest winner I've ever known. He gave me the encouragement to understand that it's my world, too, and that it's OK to feel good no matter where we came from.

Just when I get to thinking I'm great—and I do about once every two months—I remember I was honored by both houses of Congress as the new speaker on the circuit. I came in from the back of the room late. I was wearing my bank-loan suit (my sincere suit), which I always wear. It has a vest to hold my stomach in (I'm 46 and need all the help I can get.). I walked in from the back of the room, nervous. When I get nervous, I get a good grip on myself and I rock back and forth, toes to heels. When I really got nervous I broke into my Bob Newhart shtick, a nervous laugh, and I went, "Ha, ha, ha, ha, ha," because no one cared that I was there, and I finally got their attention.

As I looked out in the audience, the Senator from Massachusetts recognized me on sight for who I really am. He looked up from his seat, and he said, "Come on down." Just like Bob Barker on *The Price is Right*, he said, "Come on down."

Well, I walked down like Vince Lombardi. I was the Marlboro man in the NFL, leather-on-leather. I thought, *What do you know. I finally made it.* I walked down and I said, "Senator Kennedy and Senator Mansfield, how you gentlemen doing today?"

Senator Kennedy said, "We need some more rolls and butter here."

You don't think it happened, but it really did. They thought I was the maître d' and so did someone outside, who asked me to show them to their seats.

> ◈ **ENTREPRENEUR TIP**
>
> Waitley's anecdote is a good reminder that self-awareness is often dependent on reading the room and remembering that, sometimes, people's perceptions of you may not match your own sense of self-awareness.

WINNING

What is winning? Winning is never whining. Winning is picking up a beer can you didn't throw on the beach. Winning is coming in fourth when you came in fifth last time. Winning is treating animals like people and people like brothers and sisters. Winning is all in the attitude, no question. Talent is cheap. The world is full of talented winos on every corner. Education, you can get. Educated derelicts are wandering around. Instead, I'd give every child in the world a box of attitude for Christmas and keep it going.

The program I teach is called *Psychology of Winning: The Ten Traits of the Total Person.* I've never seen one [a total person], but if there could be one, he or she would be like this. They'd have self-awareness that the world is abundant. They'd look at the environment as a candy store that you couldn't live in a thousand years and tap out any of it. They'd look at the flowers instead of stepping on the weeds. They'd see that the abundance is there for all of us in the environment.

They'd look at their body, not like I looked at mine. In my awareness, I looked at my body as an old clunker to get me from birth to death with the least number of overhauls. I got a '33 Dodge Caravan, and if you and I went out to eat, I would eat a salad in front of you, but up in my room I've got Twinkies, Ding Dongs, and M&M's. I'm a closet eater; there's no question about it.

I thought life was a race to come in first, and I'm darn near there already. I've got some self-awareness about my body. Try it sometime.

Once, I walked into my room. I locked the door, I thought. I listened for footsteps; there weren't any. I locked my bedroom door, took off all my clothes, put a grocery bag over my head, and cut eye holes right in it. I slipped it over my head and looked at myself in front of a full-length mirror for the first time in my life. I didn't see an old friend. I looked full length at a stranger with a bag over his head, and I saw the Incredible Hulk. I gave myself a side view, and I started laughing. I gave myself a rear view, and I said, "I don't know who you are, but get dressed and get out."

Just then my wife walked in, and she said, "Ha, ha, ha!"

And I said, quickly recovering, "Trick or treat, dear."

And she said, "I'll take the trick."

She said, "Be kind to yourself. If you're going to go into a self-awareness nude-cult movement, go ahead and be nude, but don't cut eye holes in the bag. You'll like yourself better that way." But now, I know what's happening (and what was happening then): self-awareness. I've been selling myself short. The environment is a candy store. My body is a Ferrari. You're supposed to tweak and tune it to win at the Grand Prix at LeMans. It's an Apollo spacecraft. You can't fly the environment unless you feel good. You cannot *do* good unless you *feel* good.

I'm lazy. I know 500 songs but only the first four notes. If you think I know anything special, no, I don't; it's garbage in, garbage out. I'm lazy.

> ### ● ENTREPRENEUR TIP
>
> Take five minutes to do a quick self-assessment of your own self-awareness. Focus on one area of your life whether it's physical, mental, or emotional, and jot down a quick bulleted list of what you notice. You can take these mini self-awareness inventories as frequently as you like. Chart them in your journal so you can see how they change over time.

What am I afraid of? I'm afraid to win. Why? Winning is heavy. You have to act responsibly and set an example. People try to knock you off. I'm not afraid to fail. I do it every day. I'm afraid to win because winning is heavy. Self-awareness. Abundance. Moment of truth. Step back.

SELF-ESTEEM

Aside from self-awareness, self-esteem is the single most important human quality. I realize I could have been Paul Newman instead of looking like Alfred E. Neuman. I realize I'm 46. I weigh about 190 with "gusts" to 210. I realize I coulda-woulda-shoulda-mighta-oughta and if only Ida, and, someday, I'll. But now I know where the action is. If the spiritual love comes through and you feel it, then you give it away.

Why? You wouldn't know it if you didn't feel it. How could you love anyone else unless you love yourself? You couldn't. So then, self-love isn't narcissism or hedonism. Self-esteem is the single most important quality because skyjackers have none, assassins have none, criminals have none. The winners have it. Why? They want to give it away. They realize happiness is the by-product of a good life, with nothing to be sought. They're happy in building the best self in order to give it away.

I've been able to spot self-esteem early in children. Why? I raised mine the *wrong* way. I've got six children, all boys—except four girls. I want my children to be winners, so I've raised them every way I can. I've given them all the great "encouragement" a parent can. *Big boys don't cry. Don't you get angry with me. I'll give you something to cry about. Don't take the biggest piece of cake, either. That's not the way to draw a cow. Cows have bags with fingers on them. Stay inside the lines. Here, let Dad show you how to do it.*

My daughters crawled all over me at night when I was watching Walter Cronkite. I said, "Don't coddle me." How did I know it was a rejection of affection?

My daughter said, "Why don't you come out and see our store?"

I said, "I will as soon as I watch Monday Night Football." It was the last quarter. They had to go to bed. Too bad. I didn't see what they'd done. Pretty soon, I got the message [intended for me, and not for them]. I needed to grow up. Quick.

I grew up to be humble and sometimes humiliated. Why? I don't like to indulge myself in praise or feel it. On my birthday, I like to barbecue. I don't like to open my presents because I don't want people to feel so special. I've been able to spot self-esteem now growing up in two ways. People with high self-esteem never lead with their chin; they always lead with their best self, and people with high self-esteem can accept a compliment with a simple "thank you."

Here's an example. My wife and I ate out in Atlanta, Georgia, on our anniversary. Here's how you can spot self-esteem quickly. People need to understand that your little inner R2-D2 from *Star Wars* (self-image) is listening every day, making blips on the tape; it doesn't care what's right or wrong. We went the full anniversary route: waterfalls, candlelight, violins, my wife and I dressed up for each other. She looked at the waiter and stared at him. He was 28 years old; looked good, good self-esteem, good smile. He walked up and gave me his self-worth smile, which prequalified himself in advance right away in the negative. He came up and said, "What'll it be?"

I said, "Veal Diane flambé prepared at the table."

He said, "You want Veal Diane flambé'?"

I said, "That's right."

He said, "It's my first week on the job. I've never prepared anything like that. I might splatter grease all over your wife, maybe set her on fire." He said, "Why don't you order something simple from the menu? I can't do it."

I said, "What? You don't want to play the anniversary waltz for us? Is that what you said?"

He said, "No, I said don't order that stuff. I can't do it. Maybe I can get my buddy to help us. Smoke will fill the room."

I said, "I'll forget you said it, because my wife and I are easy. We wouldn't have known had you not mentioned it, and besides we just want

---

☙ ENTREPRENEUR TIP

Need to boost your self-esteem? Talk yourself into it! Take a few moments each morning to do a little positive self-talk. Think of three things you really like about yourself, then try to notice those in action as you move through your day.

to have a good time. Go ahead and try. You'll have to experiment someday, and we're easy."

He said, "What a weirdo."

He went ahead and struggled with it. I gave him the self-esteem afterward. I gave him $30 as a tip. He backed away from his self-esteem and said, "It wasn't worth that much." I took $25 right back off the tray.

He said, "It was worth more than that."

I said, "If it wasn't worth it to you, how could it be worth it to me?"

He said, "Well, I just didn't think I did that good a job."

I said, "Well, but it was worth it, wasn't it?" I laid $10 on the table, on his tip tray.

He said, "Thank you. It hurts."

I said, "It's like a gold medal that goes around your neck, isn't it?" And your shoulders go forward, and you pull them back and say thank you, and your little R2-D2 from *Star Wars* inside your head goes, *Huh! I didn't think he was worth it, either, but he said thanks.* I guess he accepted it.

I laid another $10 on it, and he said, "Thank you very much."

I laid down the other $5. He said, "Thank you."

I said, "By the way, winners never prequalify in advance, in the negative, and always say thank you to accept the value paid every day."

◉ ENTREPRENEUR ACTION ITEM
Know the Eight Habits of Highly Effective Entrepreneurs

Dr. Waitley's approach to winning with self-awareness and self-esteem puts an exclamation point on the idea that most often success comes from within. Let's explore that further and link it to entrepreneurship. One measure of entrepreneurial success is your efficacy as a leader. Effectiveness comes down to producing desired results. The most successful entrepreneurs have mastered being effective because it makes them work smarter, eliminating unnecessary effort and wasted time. Success cannot happen with any consistency when approached in a lazy, haphazard, hit-or-miss fashion. Effectiveness is rooted in discipline and routine, not talent or genius. Successful entrepreneurs make sure to be detailed, organized, and fully prepared before executing any goal or plan. Self-awareness and self-esteem are the programs running in the background of your mind (like the R2-D2 Waitley mentions) that help make it all happen.

So what does that look like in practice? Here are eight characteristics of effective entrepreneurs that are connected to Waitley's winning mindset:

Visionary Mindset

Successful entrepreneurs spend a significant amount of time thinking, creating, and visioning. Being innovative comes naturally to all of us if we can discipline ourselves to enjoy the process of being in constant discovery. A successful entrepreneur's most powerful asset is their imagination. The most effective entrepreneurs dare to dream, act, and turn their dreams into a reality. This visionary quality sets them apart from those who do not dare to dream as big. Standout entrepreneurs do not see a limit to their creativity, success, or ability to make money. They also have a positive and lasting impact on others and involve themselves in new ventures.

Embrace the Day Early

The most effective entrepreneurs are early risers. They support the belief that the early bird gets the worm. They start their day visualizing what they want to achieve and speak affirmations of success over their mindset. Many also start their day with some form of physical activity. It's the method they use to wake themselves up, and get their blood pumping and their mind alert and active. Getting up early and getting a jump on their day allows them to get into the office before others arrive. This gives them some time to settle themselves, collect their thoughts, and generate lists of priorities to most efficiently organize and tackle their day.

Scheduled

One of the easiest ways successful entrepreneurs increase effectiveness is by being scheduled. They live a schedule based on putting their responsibilities first and leisure activities second. Socializing is important and life-giving. Successful entrepreneurs recognize the value in getting out to be around people, not just for the human interaction and feelings of interconnectedness, but because being around others reduces stress and increases innovation. The most effective entrepreneurs schedule social time at the end of their day when work pressures are off. When responsibilities are put first, this type of discipline helps successful entrepreneurs enjoy their free time unencumbered by nagging responsibilities that were not met during the day.

Honor the Power of Sleep

To be effective, successful entrepreneurs appreciate the importance of sleep. The more sleep they get, the sharper, more emotionally available, and mentally on point they tend to be. A lack of sleep creates an increase in emotional reactivity and a decrease in frustration tolerance, which contributes to another night of poor sleep. It's a horrible cycle. If poor sleeping patterns are left unmanaged, effectiveness and success become impossible.

Simplicity

Simplicity is the secret weapon successful entrepreneurs swear by to increase their effectiveness. They live nearly obsessively by simple yet practical routines. Creating simple routines helps them avoid taking on workloads that are beyond what they can reasonably handle. They are the most productive when they are not too overwhelmed with stress. So they set protective and firm limits around themselves and their time, understanding even superheroes need a day off.

Prioritize Journaling

One of the easiest ways to increase effectiveness is to develop the habit of journaling. The most effective entrepreneurs put pen to paper and write down what is important to them, the things that were good and bad during their day, and ideas on how they can improve. They write lists and goals, express their gratitude, and sometimes write simply to vent their frustrations. Journaling calms the emotions caused by stress or conflict. It provides a much-needed disconnect from the daily grind of consistent talking, emailing, and other distractions resulting from electronic devices that never allow us to fully unplug. Successful entrepreneurs value participating in an active dialogue with their inner critic as it helps them to transmute this negative voice into a positive coaching voice that is all about overcoming odds. Entrepreneurs are the most effective when they're strategizing ways to beat a challenge.

Flexible

As important as routine is, successful entrepreneurs also understand how imperative it is that they are flexible enough to pivot on demand in response to unforeseen or changing circumstances. Being flexible enough to change direction greatly increases their chances at success, and it also enhances their own learning, growth, and education. The routines they live by are simple by design because this simplicity makes it easy for them to maintain their life and career no matter their circumstances. Effective entrepreneurs make it a habit to only need the bare essentials. This increases their productivity because their setup to work and communicate doesn't require anything special from them to be effective, whether they are at the beach or in the office.

Curious

The most effective entrepreneurs view boredom as the great success killer, which is why they make sure never to be bored. They happily spend endless hours working and doing what they love. They have made it a habit to be open and curious about everything in life and in their field of work. This curiosity keeps them asking questions and generating ideas for what their next steps are going to be. Because they choose to remain open and curious, it is impossible to drain their creative reservoirs. Curiosity is just another aspect that contributes to their effectiveness.

Do you have any of these characteristics? How does your self-awareness help you identify what you have inside you as an entrepreneur and what you can work on to level up your winning game?

CHAPTER TWO

Every Problem Has a Solution

Dr. Norman Vincent Peale

D r. Norman Vincent Peale was a minister who spent many years at the Marble Collegiate Church in New York City until his death in 1993 at age 95. Dr. Peale was also a bestselling author, whose themes radiated around the power of positive thinking.

One of Peale's books, *The Power of Positive Thinking*, was first published in 1960 and is still popular today. It has sold over 7 million copies and has been published in 15 different languages. This book has been credited with restoring the faith of millions of people.

Peale also gave a speech titled "Every Problem has a Solution" to a live audience of thousands, which focused on the principle of having a positive attitude. In this selection from that speech, Peale's background in storytelling and is evident as he makes his case for the power of positivity.

❦ ❦ ❦

THE SOLUTION IS RIGHT IN FRONT OF YOU

The street crowds in an English Cathedral town were going about their ordinary activities. Suddenly, someone spotted a woman who'd crawled out on a narrow ledge near the top of the central tower of the cathedral. Policemen quickly climbed the tower and attempted to bring her back. A minister came and prayed with her, pleading with her to let him talk with her about whatever was on her mind that inspired this last, desperate act. A great crowd gathered below, hushed and horrified. After some 30 minutes of indecision, she flung herself from the tower down onto the street. Now nobody knows what problem the woman had that drove her to this desperation. But there was one thing she apparently didn't know or to which she gave no concern. It's a great, powerful truth, and had she known it, she wouldn't have thrown herself off the tower. She didn't know that every problem contains its own solution.

One of the wisest statements I have heard in many a day is one that I have quoted before, I'm quite sure. It deserves to be and is a classic. This quote comes from Stanley Arnold, one of the top idea men in the country. He services a number of the great industries of the United States with sales and merchandising ideas, and his services come very highly recommended. Why? Because he's a thinker. He thinks up ideas, and he knows how to praise them.

Now this one is worth its weight in gold if he could sell it. Every problem, he says, contains the seeds of its own solution, not the seeds of its dissolution, but the seeds of its *solution*. I've quoted that before and perhaps it ought to be repeated from time to time until at last the thought, the truth, really grabs us. That whenever you have a problem, buried right at the heart of this problem, however difficult it may seem to be, is the solution thereof.

When you're talking about thinking and ideas and truth, you're in the right place right here in this church because the Bible is quite a book. Every smart thing that exists is right here in these pages. It is full of ideas that are as modern as tomorrow morning's newspaper. The 119th Psalm, the 18th verse, is one of them. It goes something like this: *Open my eyes that I may behold wondrous things out of thy law.* What law? Why the basic law of the universe, not the law of aerodynamics, not the law of mechanics—the law of the spirit of the mentality. Open my eyes that I may see wondrous things out of thy law.

One of these wondrous things is (and it is truly a wondrous thing) that every problem that you or I can have contains the seeds of its own solution. Right up here in your head is to be found the answer to everything. Epictetus, the ancient thinker [a Greek Stoic philosopher] said, "When you shut your door and darken your room, always remember you are not alone. God is in you and, therefore, genius is within you." What a truth. So what's your problem? Hold it out there in front of you. Give it a good look over. Rip it apart. Break it up. Get to the center of it. Dissect it. Analyze it. Right at the center of it, buried like a gem, is its solution.

"Well," you say, "that's great, but how do you do it?"

I like to suggest three principles for so doing. First, think—really think. Second, believe—really believe. Third, pray—really pray [which Peale explains later is more akin to a form of relaxation or meditation]. Now there you have three dynamic principles, and with those principles, you can, I do believe (in fact, I know), find an answer. The end—the right answer to any human problem.

THINK YOUR WAY TO A SOLUTION

Let's take that first one: Think, really think. Let me ask you something. How long has it been since you *really* thought? I might ask that of myself. When did I last think? I don't like to think, do you? It's painful. It's one of the most painful things known to man. Thinking, deep thinking—we shrink from it. We like to be relieved of the necessity of it, so we think off the top of our heads. The trouble with those thoughts off the top of the head is that they do not go down into the depths, so you have to agonizingly think. But when one gets over the first hump of thinking and gets into the area where it's creative, actually it's a delightful and inspiring experience.

Be "Quick," not "Dead"

John Burroughs was one of the greatest naturalists that this country ever produced, probably THE greatest. [In fact, Burroughs was very active in the U.S. conservation movement.] He said that there are just two classes of people in the world. He said he doesn't mean men and women, those two classes. Or young and old or rich and poor or black and white or Republicans or Democrats. He said those aren't the two classes that he refers to, but the two classes in his mind are what he calls the "quick" and the "dead." The *quick* are people who look at the world and see it. They are people who listen to the world and hear it. They get a message from it. The quick are people who are sensitive, sensitized. They send up an antenna. They get the meaning of the world. They see what they're looking at. They're alive; they're alert; they're vibrant. Those are the quick. The other people aren't dead *physically*, but they're dead from the standpoint of sensitivity. They live on the surface. So there are two classes—the quick and the dead, and the quick see the wondrous things [in the world].

There are so many illustrations of this, but let me give you one. The other day my wife presented me with all the sermons that I have preached over 38 years in this church. She had them bound in nice volumes: number one, number two, and so on beginning in 1932. That's a lot of sermons, and she put them up in my office. I don't know whether she put them there for enlightenment or for decorative purposes, but the color of the books fits in with the décor, you might say.

I was very impressed by these volumes, so I thought I'd look inside and see if I could find anything inside that was impressive also. Now bear in mind I was reading my own sermons, which shows to what extremity I was reduced. But I picked up the volume for 1951 and I read one of the sermons there, and you know, it wasn't half bad. I found an illustration there, which I had long since forgotten but which is really a beauty as to how you think through a problem, a tough problem. I know that when I talk this way I have people saying, "Look, you don't know how tough my problem is," which shows that you're thinking, but you're thinking negatively.

This was the story. It seems that there was a couple by the name of Mr. and Mrs. Hustead, and they lived in a little town in South Dakota called Wall, population I think some 500 or 600. The time when this story was laid was back at a time when there was a great drought all over that western area of the country. There had been days upon end without any rain, and the soil was pulverized finely. The winds would catch it and sweep it in great dust clouds, and it formed what was known as the great dust bowl. This caused one of the greatest migrations in American history, of people who no longer could get any value out of a farm. Farm prices fell to nothing. People were ruined. They were impoverished. There was poverty everywhere all over that part of the country.

The Husteads ran a drug store in a little town in such a setting as this, and you can imagine the drug business wasn't going very well. So they were sitting there one day when the temperature was 100 in the shade with no customers coming into their store and they were facing financial ruin, although they never admitted that they were. They knew that somewhere there was an idea that would help them. They sat in the front windows with their chin in their hands watching people go along on the highway which hadn't yet been hard surfaced, amid great rolling clouds of dust (there was no car air conditioning at this time). The windows were up and the dust was sweeping in from these cars, and Mrs. Hustead said, "Here is the proposition. We have something for these people in this store. How can we make them know that we have something for them so that the two of us will get together?" But they [the travelers] went by rapidly through this little one-horse town. Now, I have developed this story at great length in order that you can see a problem in which you would seem to think there wasn't a ray of hope. But this woman had great faith. She opened her eyes to see wondrous things.

So she prayed. She believed, she thought, and she asked herself, "What would those people out there at this moment with 100 degrees in the shade in this dust rather have than anything else?" And the answer came to her out of her head where she was thinking. What they would love to have is a cold, big glass of ice water. So she told her husband to make signs, and they went up for 100 miles on either side of this village. The signs were right on the highway. They went 50 miles on either side of the village, 25 miles on either side of the village, and 10 miles on either side of the village, and they put up big signs that said, "To all passing motorists, there is a free, tall, frosted glass of pure, cold, delicious ice water awaiting you at the Wall Drugstore, Wall, South Dakota. Hold on till you can get to Wall." They even went so far as to go as far east as Albany, New York, and they put up a sign for a free glass of ice water at Wall, South Dakota, 1,725 miles further on. Did customers flock to the drugstore? Of course they did! It wasn't long until Mr. and Mrs. Hustead had 25 clerks not only handing out ice water but selling their merchandise as well.

◈ ENTREPRENEUR TIP

Don't underestimate the power of brainstorming when you need to think of possible solutions to your problem. Getting your team around the conference room table and opening your minds to multiple possible solutions (no matter how far-fetched) just might open the door to one that really works.

The point is that we won't usually acknowledge that there's a *possibility* of a solution, and you may even get a little irritated if anybody tells you that your problem is not without solution. There's a solution to any problem. It doesn't come easy. Of course not. What you have to do is to practice those three principles. Think, really think. Believe, really believe, and pray, really pray. And the result will be that your eyes are opened and you see wondrous things.

BELIEVE YOU CAN OVERCOME OBSTACLES

The second thing is to believe, really believe. The question is: How deeply do we believe? Do we again believe only with the surface of the mind? There's a statement somewhere [that says] if, with all your heart, you truly seek me, you will find me. Nobody ever made anything great out of their life who didn't do it with all their heart.

I remember years ago talking to a celebrity whose name would be known to everybody. I know she had had a great deal of trouble in her life. I said, "How come you keep at this with such enthusiasm?"

"Why," she said, "I do it because I love it. I give my whole self to it." And she did. She threw everything she had into it. If with all your heart you give yourself to your business, to your children, to your marriage, to your future, and to your hopes, you're going to come out with something that's lasting and strong. Believe—that's it!

I once addressed a luncheon of the National Association of Manufacturers at the Waldorf Astoria Grand Ballroom. A huge crowd of some of the great businesspeople of this country was there. I got into a conversation there with a man who said, "There's a man here you'd like."

I said, "I seem to like all of the people I'm meeting here."

"Well," he said, "this man's a special case. This man has had trouble, poverty, resistance, and difficulties, but despite all that, he has created a great enterprise."

So naturally, I hunted him up. I had only two minutes with him, maybe not quite that. I said to him, "What's the great secret of your successful performance?" And he began to disclaim it. I said, "No, give me the facts. I know you've done a great job. Tell me, how did you do it? How did you lift this business up to where it is?"

"Well," he said, "In the first place, I believed in it. I believed that this business is necessary for the welfare of the American people. It was hard going, but I just believed it into greatness." And that phrase is likewise worthy to be a classic: *I believed it into greatness.* So whatever your job is, believe it into greatness. If you have a child or a young person under your wing, just

> ### ⚜ ENTREPRENEUR TIP
>
> Believing in yourself or your business is a great feeling. So why not share the wealth? Make a practice of sharing the power of belief with your employees, clients, and colleagues. Showing others you believe in them goes a long way toward fostering morale and a healthy company culture.

believe them into greatness. Believe everything into greatness. Think—really think. Believe—really believe. There's no limit to the power of belief.

I heard a story not long ago about a little incident that happened a good many years ago out in the Midwest in a farmhouse. This boy, 17 years old, was desperately ill. He had pneumonia. In those days pneumonia was a sinister disease; still nothing to trifle with now. But now we have drugs that can fight it successfully, but there were no such drugs in those days. If you did survive it, it was because you had basic good health, or because you asked God to give you life. Medicine in those days could only cope with it partially.

Well, it was late at night, and this boy was lying there in a coma, and the doctor said, "Really, this boy is so healthy and strong and his lungs respond to a certain degree that I see no reason why this boy should die. I'm baffled by it." He sat there in his shirtsleeves studying the boy, the clock on the wall ticking, the parents huddling together arm in arm, anxious, their little children frightened, the neighbors concerned. Finally the doctor said, "What this boy needs is a transfusion."

Everyone immediately said, "We'll give our blood."

"No," he said, "it isn't a blood transfusion that he needs. It's a faith transfusion. It's the desire to live. In some way he's killing himself because the faith isn't there to pull him through."

What a doctor. He said, "If something doesn't happen to him in the way of a transfusion like that, he'll die before morning." There was an old farmer there, and he had his Bible in his hand. Great big gnarled hands struggling with the earth, he cradled his Bible lovingly in his hand. This farmer was a believer. He was a simple man. He took the Bible as it was. He took the promises of God as they were. He just accepted them. He didn't doubt them. He believed in them. He had the faith of a little child, and when the doctor said the boy needed a faith transfusion, he drew near to the patient, put his mouth close down to his ear, and he started reading him great passages out of the Bible with the thought that he was driving them below and beneath his conscious mind into his unconscious mind, trying to reach the center of control.

The hours passed. He read on. The clock continued to tick. The doctor paced the floor. On and on, hour after hour, he drove these healing thoughts into this boy's consciousness, until finally when the first faint streaks of dawn came suddenly, the boy gave a sigh. His eyes opened. He looked at the man and all the people in the room and gave them a big healthy smile and fell into a deep untroubled, normal sleep. The doctor felt his pulse, looked for the vital signs, and with tears in his eyes said, "The transfusion has been made. The crisis has passed. The boy will live." And he did live, saved by what? By faith and prayer and thought. They found that the problem had its solution right within itself as all problems do—the solution was believing in something.

> ⚇ **ENTREPRENEUR TIP**
>
> This story shows that belief in something helps you overcome obstacles. The author's experience as a preacher shines through in this example, obviously, but the real takeaway (regardless of what you believe in) is that focusing forward on something more powerful than yourself is a key to overcoming what's in your way.

RELAX TO WIN

One of the greatest skills to learn in these busy and hectic days is how to relax. Real power for handling your job, for running your home, for improving your personal relationships, comes from a mind that is free of tension. When you learn how to relax, your creative power will come through. Your energy will be conserved and real accomplishment will be the result. So let us spend a few minutes together thinking about techniques for cultivating this great art of relaxing.

I would say that the first step is to learn how to train and drain your mind, because you have to train your mind to drain it. The average person, before retiring for the day, usually empties their pockets onto a dresser or maybe a desk. Personally, I rather enjoy standing over a wastebasket during this process because I just love to see how many things I can get rid of. Things like notes, memos, scraps of paper, completed self-directions, maybe even knickknacks I've picked up. With great relief, I deposit all the items I possibly can in the wastepaper basket. It occurred to me one night that it would be a good idea to empty my mind as I emptied my pockets. You see, during the day we pick up many mental odds and ends: a little worry, a little resentment, a few annoyances, some irritations, perhaps even some guilty reactions. Every night all these things should be drained off, for unless they're eliminated, they will accumulate.

Now, how do you drain your thoughts? I suggest that you think of your mind as a sink with a stopper in the bottom. Mentally remove the stopper and imaginatively see the mass of soiled material disappear down the drain. Then mentally replace the stopper and fill the mind with clean thoughts. You must be very careful in performing this process never to take a thought back. When you have drained an unhealthy thought out of your mind, conceive of it as gone for good. If your mind attempts to reach out for the old thought, stop it at once by saying, "That thought is gone forever. I removed it, and I will not take it back."

There are other metaphors you can use to clear your mind. One night I came home to find my wife, ever the perfect housekeeper, experimenting with some new appliances for her vacuum cleaner. She showed me a long arm attachment with which dust could be sucked out of hidden corners. While admiring this mechanical gadget, it occurred to me that a similar mechanism could be employed to draw or suck dust out of our thoughts. So I developed, for myself, what you might call a vacuum cleaner prayer [or meditation]. It goes like this: *Draw now from the unseen crannies and crevices of my mind, the dust of the world which has settled in there.* Try this. The resulting sense of mental cleanness will, for sure, add to your inner peace.

Another method is figuratively and imaginatively to reach into your mind as though you could put your fingers into your brain and lift out unhappy, tense thoughts one by one. As you imagine yourself doing this, affirm in this manner: *I am now taking out and throwing away that fear, that prejudice, that*

◉ ENTREPRENEUR TIP

Simple meditation is a terrific way to center your thoughts and prepare for the day to come or even to step out of your busy day and reconnect with your thoughts. You don't need a special room or complicated process. Just find a quiet spot, empty your mind, focus on breathing, and just be for a few minutes. Then your mind is clear and ready to tackle the next thing on your to-do list.

resentment or that recollection. Then, when the mind is thus emptied, affirm as follows: *I am now putting pure thoughts into my mind.*

Simplify Your Night

Perhaps at this point, I should suggest that you don't take tomorrow to bed with you, ever. I knew a man who complained of being a poor sleeper. We analyzed his daily and nightly habits and discovered that after he got to bed, he took a pad and pencil and made a series of notes about what he was going to do the next day. He planned out tomorrow, making an outline of each problem or responsibility that was to be handled. He actually prided himself on this efficient method he had developed and considered it a unique procedure. He placed the pad and pencil on his night table and would often reach for them in the darkness, adding additional memos that his restless mind supplied. He told with pride how well he had mastered the skill of writing legibly in the darkness. Why couldn't he sleep? Simply because he was taking tomorrow to bed with him. So, never do that. Now I do believe in efficiency, of course. In fact, one of my mottos is: *Plan your work and work your plan.* But there is a time and a place for all things, and in bed, ready to go to sleep, is certainly not the time to plan the next day. In fact, as one approaches the hours of rest, certain preparations will prove beneficial.

During the last hour before retiring, deliberately prevent your mind from being agitated by any kind of problem. The cares, responsibilities, and decisions of life should be put aside for the night so that mind, soul, and body may be refreshed and renewed by sound, healthful sleep. Let your mind, as far as possible, go into neutral. Affirm it in this manner: *I now cease mental consideration of this problem.* Visualize all matters as being put aside. Think of any problem as being deeply dropped into subconscious to quietly simmer, you might say, until morning. When you take it up again, believe it or not, it may have solved itself. Spend the last hour preliminary to sleep in light and homey conversation with your loved ones or friends. If you live alone, select an entertaining radio or television program or read a carefree story. Nothing ponderous.

After reading, spend a few minutes in relaxed meditation. Conceive of the words that you have read as seeping deeply into your mind, and picture them as spreading a spiritual bond throughout your entire being. In this quiescent state, allow your body to adjust itself further in muscular relaxation. As you undress your body to prepare for bed, also undress your mind. You wouldn't think, would you, of climbing into bed fully dressed? But how often we get into bed with our minds encumbered by all manner of unhappy thoughts. Drop off one by one these weights that the mind has carried throughout the day so that it will be free of pressure and as comfortable as your unclothed body.

Before getting into bed, stand at the window and reflect on the beauty of the night. Behold the moon sailing high in the heavens lighting up the clouds in silvery radiance. Contemplate the stars, or perhaps watch the snow slanting toward the earth or drifting high against the fence, or listen to the heavy padded quietness of the fog. Or put your head out the window and let the rain fall against your face for a moment. Let the beauty and the mystery of the world make itself felt in your thoughts. This type of thing will absorb in consciousness and make you peaceful.

Avoid Self-Obsession

Another step in relaxing is this: Don't wear yourself out with yourself. Now, what do I mean by that? Simply this. Much tiredness is the result of extreme self-preoccupation, introspection, and concern about comforts, prerogatives, or position. All these things consume a large share of one's energy. I've observed that people who have the time and strength to do things in a big way always give the least attention to themselves. Their wants are reduced to a minimum. They give themselves just enough time to care for physical requirements and to dress neatly. The main bulk of their time and energy is thus available to do the important jobs in life. So make a list of all the little things you do about your own person every day, and see how much of this minutia you can lop off.

I would suggest that you practice becoming systematic. There's a friend of mine who's a very systematic man, although he once wasn't that way at all, but now he is. He lays out his underwear, socks, shirt, and tie and he decides on his suit for the morning before going to bed. "Like a fireman," he says, "I get into my regalia in half the time it formerly required."

I would also suggest that you avoid obsessing. Obsessions probably cause the greatest strain on energy of any personal disability. It is quite impossible to become practiced in relaxed living and enjoy restful rest until one overcomes those compulsive neuroses of an obsessional nature, which drive and harass people and make them really victims of life itself, victims of themselves. For example, I recall one poor fellow who felt that he had to perform a complicated ritual every day, and this was the ritual. He always went back to the sink three times to be sure the water was turned off. Then he tried the door three times to be sure it was locked. He constantly worried that unless he did this or that or some other thing that some hazy, terrible thing would happen. This poor fellow used up so much energy on these obsessions that he was a tired, worn-out man even before he tried to do his work. He was pretty successful, but he did it at the expenditure of an enormous amount of energy. Many people have these obsessions. What is the cure? Well, this man confessed, emptied out, and received forgiveness for some wrongdoings he had committed that he was trying mentally to cover up. These sins festering in the subconscious had created a guilty feeling and stimulated the unconscious, creating a persistent conviction that he should be punished. So by doing these things, this ritual, he was actually unconsciously punishing himself. He was actually pursuing himself to inflict punishment upon himself. A deep spiritual experience cured him of all his foolishness. He received forgiveness and forgave himself by accepting mercy with gratitude. So many people are tired because such emotional illnesses drive them to irrational compensation for wrongdoing. So get your guilt feeling cleared up. Then and then only can you truly relax and be restful.

Practice Visualization

Another technique, which I use constantly, and I've found it really very wonderful, I call *memorized peacefulness*. One time in the midst of activities, which I had foolishly allowed to become hectic, I went down to Atlantic City. From my window I could look out directly upon the sea as it washed gently on soft shores of sand. It was very quieting to behold this scene. The day was overcast with drifting fog and clouds. Imperturbably, the sea rolled shoreward with its deep-throated roar and ceaseless but perfect rhythm. Clean spew blew from its wave crest. Over the beach and climbing high against the sky and then sliding down the wind with ineffable grace, seagulls soared and dived. Everything in this scene was graceful, beautiful, and conducive to serenity.

Its benign peacefulness began to lay a healing, clouding touch upon me, and I began to relax. I happened to close my eyes, and when I did so, I discovered a wonderful thing: that I could still visualize the scene just as I had beheld it. There it was as clear-cut in my mind as when actually viewed by the eye.

It occurred to me then that the reason I could see it with my eyes closed was because my memory had absorbed it and was able to reproduce it in detail. Why then, I reasoned, could I not live again and again in this scene of quiet beauty even though bodily absent from the place? I began, therefore, the practice of deliberately visualizing quiet scenes of beauty in which I had once lived. Sometimes in the midst of active work I have found it profitable to stop for a minute or two and bring up out of memory's storehouse scenes that had impressed me by their peace and loveliness, and experience, once again, the remarkable power of the quiet to soothe and to relax.

I have found that when sleep comes with difficulty, I can actually induce slumber by visualizing out of memory scenes of quietness and peace. Lying in a relaxed manner in my bed, I practice going back as far as I can remember and recollect one by one truly peaceful experiences in my life, such as the time I gazed upon Mt. Blanc when the vast mountain was bathed in full moonlight. Or the radiant sun-kissed morning when our great white ship dropped anchor in the incredible blue waters off Waikiki Beach in Honolulu. Or that mystic evening when I first watched the purple shadows fill the Grand Canyon to overflowing with hush. Or when I watched the sunlight sift through ancient maple trees onto a green lawn on a summer afternoon at my farm home. And I traversed these marvelous

⚜ ENTREPRENEUR TIP

Having a tough time sleeping? Practice some visualization or meditation techniques before hitting the sheets. Envision yourself at peace, surrounded by an environment that you find relaxing and appealing. Or, envision yourself accomplishing the goals you have set out for the next day. You can also do a short meditation to quiet the mind. There are some useful apps available to help you power down through meditation, including Calm, Headspace, and Insight Timer.

scenes of beauty and peace through the power of memory to recreate them. I drifted into a sound and untroubled sleep. So practice the memorized peacefulness. Now and then, let go of your cares and problems of the day and wander in memory among the most beautiful places and scenes in which you have ever lived. This will quiet you. It's bound to, and as you yield yourself to the benign power of quiet visualization, you will find rest and relaxation that will be deep and lasting.

Practice Selective Forgetfulness

As a counterpart to memorized peacefulness, I also suggest that you become an expert forgetter. Practicing the art of forgetting has remarkable power to relax and relieve strain. Some people complain that they have trouble memorizing. Well, far more have trouble forgetting, inasmuch as many breakdowns result from overburdening the mind with unhappy memories of failure or frustration. For them, the unburdening process of forgetting becomes of tremendous importance.

Many people lie in bed at night remembering what somebody said about them or did to them. They are hauntingly agitated by the recollection of something left undone or done poorly. As a result of this unpleasant cogitation, their minds, made miserably nervous, probe back into the past and they dwell on old things, old sins, old sorrows, and old unhappiness. Then the mind flips restlessly from one misery center to another, somewhat after the manner of the bee, except that it's not taking honey from beautiful flowers of pleasant episodes, but rather sipping dissatisfaction from the rank weeds of past experience.

A superlative aid to mental health, and especially becoming master of the art of forgetting, is forgetting those things which are behind and reaching forward to those things which are before you. Repeat this to yourself when your mind tends to dwell on unhappy things. This will help you to forget, and the extent to which you master the skill of forgetting, you will really enjoy untroubled and energy-renewing sleep. Such forgetting, of course, is not a negative but a positive process. It is the effective forcing of something destructive from the thoughts by a process of displacement. So, let go of every unhealthy thought. Cast everyone out, let peaceful thoughts into your mind, and have love in your heart toward everyone. Do all this, really do it, and you will become a master of the great skill of relaxation.

◈ ENTREPRENEUR ACTION ITEM
Rewire Your Brain to Be More Positive

Dr. Peale's approach to positivity (and success, of course) is one that you can apply to your own life experiences, no matter your background or belief system. As he mentioned, putting yourself in a positive mindset can often be a matter of reimagining how you think, believe, and practice being mindful. It's almost as if you can rewire your brain to leave the negative behind or, at the very least, use those negative thoughts as a jumping-off point for a new, more positive way of thinking. Whether you realize it or not, the negative experiences you have lived through often influence your decisions. Your brain learns from difficult situations and painful memories, and these experiences get sealed into your brain.

Your brain naturally wants to do whatever it can to protect you by avoiding a recurrence of the negative experience. However, continually focusing on the negative can hinder our ability to find the positive and live a happy life.

Success is based on recognizing and going after opportunities as they present themselves—and that often requires having the inner fortitude to take a chance and navigate difficult waters. The more you exude positivity, the better your chances of finding lasting success and happiness. All it takes is a little training and focus, and you can rewire your brain toward the positive. Here are some tips from *Entrepreneur* that you can practice along with Dr. Peale's method:

Release Your Inner Negativity

If you allow yourself to dwell on the negative, then habitual skepticism will run your life and influence your decisions. You are effectively resigning yourself to a cycle of hesitation and distrust. It is hard, if not impossible, to build success when you have resigned yourself to negativity. The first step is to let your negativity go. It's time to focus on the affirmative. Take control of your mind and direct it toward the positive. You can start doing this by deliberately and frequently centering your thoughts on things that make you happy. Stop letting negatives limit your potential and drag you down. Start consciously taking a different approach to your thinking. One simple tip is to spend a moment calming your mind when you are feeling frazzled, stressed, or distracted. Slow things down. Take a few deep breaths and empty your mind of negative thoughts. Focus on filling your lungs with air. Now you are ready for a positive reboot.

Retrain Your Brain

Even after years of subconsciously focusing on the negative, it is possible to retrain your brain to perceive and focus on the positive. The idea is to recognize and center your thoughts on the silver linings that are embedded in any negative situation. The first step is to become aware of your thinking patterns. Start paying more attention to the flow of your thoughts. Is your brain preoccupied by constantly focusing on negative outcomes? Are you stuck in a loop of cynical thinking? Recognize that negative thinking isn't going to support you in creating long-term success. You need a balanced mind as you decide on which opportunities are the best to take.

The next step is to retrain your brain to see positive patterns. Instead of scrutinizing a situation to spot the negatives, we need to teach our brains to redirect our thoughts and scan for the positives. One simple way to begin doing this is to scan for three daily positive things. Every day, make a list of three good things that happened to you and reflect on what caused them to happen. Focus on the little wins you have each day and use those to empower and motivate yourself.

Pivot from Negative Thoughts

Once you recognize that you are caught in a continuous loop of negative reoccurring thoughts, it's time to break free by pivoting. Ask yourself what the opposite of the negative thought is. If you were to turn 180 degrees away from this antagonistic thinking, where would you find yourself? Focus on thinking about something from a positive perspective. Practice visualizing a more positive outcome. Then think about the steps you need to take to make that happen. If you tend to be anxious or apprehensive, pay attention to when you are feeling that way. What causes those emotions? When you feel yourself slipping into a negative cycle of anxiety or worry, remind yourself that these negative thoughts are holding you back from making positive choices in your life. Consider how you can reframe your thoughts into a more positive perspective. Find a confident and assertive alternative to a negative impulse.

Recognize that your mind will want to slip back into old patterns, and remind yourself that you're reconditioning yourself to have positive thoughts and take positive actions. Once you develop the habit of pivoting toward the positive, your brain will become predisposed to doing so.

Pay It Forward

When we are nice to others—when we engage in acts of kindness and make others feel good—we boost our own happiness. Even small acts that make others smile can bring us joy. Doing something nice is also a powerful way to halt a negativity loop. For instance, you may be feeling anxious about an upcoming meeting or stressed about a recent interaction with a friend or colleague, and your usual pattern of thinking is to worry about it. Instead of fretting, try doing something compassionate for another person. You'll find that taking a moment to do a small favor, buy someone a cup of coffee, or help a stranger out can give you a little boost. It's like an instant shot of happiness. Use those positive feelings to channel your thinking into a positive pattern.

Bring Positivity into the Present

To truly reprogram your mind to be more positive, you have to bring positivity into your everyday life. You have to focus on having a positive outlook in your present moment. Not tomorrow. Not next week. Right now. You can do this through the practice of mindfulness, which is being aware of your thoughts and feelings in the present moment. It's about recognizing your emotions, what your body is sensing and what you are thinking about, and allowing these sensations to occur without judging them.

You can then harness this awareness to redirect your thoughts. Once you get into the habit of mindfulness, you are no longer allowing your subconscious mind to drive your decisions. You are teaching your brain to sense when you are slipping into negativity and take action toward the positive. It allows you to focus your thoughts and attention toward a more balanced and positive approach. To help redirect your thoughts, try writing down a list of questions you can ask yourself to bring positivity into your present moment. Here are some examples:

- What can I feel grateful about right now?
- What can I do right now that is fun or gives me joy?
- How can I demonstrate love or gratitude right now?
- What is something I can do to surprise someone or give someone else happiness right now?

As you get into the habit of continually checking in with yourself and directing your thoughts toward the positive, it will eventually become second nature.

CHAPTER THREE

Theory of Compensation

Ralph Waldo Emerson

With comments by W. Clement Stone

R alph Waldo Emerson was an American essayist, lecturer, and poet in the mid-19th century. He wrote about such topics as self-reliance, nature, conduct of life, and representative men. The philosophical movement called the transcendentalist movement centered on Emerson as well. The transcendentalist movement taught people to view the objects in the world as small versions of the whole universe and to trust their individual intuitions.

The theory of compensation that Emerson wrote about was often referred to by Napoleon Hill. In one remark, Hill said,

"The best compensation for doing things is the ability to do more." The law of compensation simply means that each person is compensated in the manner in which he or she has contributed. It can also be known as the principle of sowing and reaping.

The essay "Compensation" was first published in 1841 and played a major role in Napoleon Hill's writings on success. Look for comments sprinkled throughout by W. Clement Stone, father of the Positive Mental Attitude (PMA) movement, to provide additional insight and application.

✦ ✦ ✦

A NOTE FROM W. CLEMENT STONE

For ten years, beginning in 1952, I managed Napoleon Hill, the author of *Think and Grow Rich*. Nate Libermann, a manufacturers' representative, was one of the members of our first "Science of Success" course. He was a generous, gentle, kindly, and good man. Nate was a student of philosophy and had a keen interest in modern, inspirational, and self-help action books, such as Napoleon Hill's *Think and Grow Rich*. He had developed a particular interest in the functioning of the conscious and subconscious mind. I can hear him tell me, "Share with others a part of what you possess that is good and desirable." And I shall never forget his statement, "When you share with another ideas or ideals, you give them away, but you still keep them for yourself." It was Nate Lieberman who first introduced me to Emerson, when he gave me and every member of the class Ralph Waldo Emerson's *Essays*. Over the years, he shared with me many additional books, such as Charles Baudouin's *Suggestion and Auto Suggestion*, Thomas J. Hudson's *The Law of Psychic Phenomena*, and Joseph Marie Jacquard's *Invention and the Unconscious*. Emerson, however, was his favorite author, and "Compensation" was his favorite essay. I think you will greatly benefit from it.

COMPENSATION

My name is Ralph Waldo Emerson. Ever since I was a boy, I wished to write a discourse on compensation. For it seemed to me, when very young, that on this subject, life was ahead of theology, and the people knew more than the preachers taught. The documents from which the doctrine is to be drawn charmed my fancy by their endless variety and lay always before me even in sleep, for they are the tools in our hands, the bread in our basket, the transactions of the street, the farm and the dwelling house, the greetings, the relations, the debts and credits, the influence of character, the nature and endowment of all men. It seemed to me, also, that in it might be shown men a ray of divinity, the present action of the soul of this world clean from all vestige of tradition. And so the heart of man might be bathed by an inundation of eternal love, conversing with that which he knows was always and always must be because it really is now. It appeared moreover that if this doctrine could be stated in terms with any resemblance to those bright intuitions in which this truth is sometimes revealed to us, it would be a star in many dark hours and crooked passages in our journey that would not suffer us to lose our way. I was lately confirmed in these desires by hearing a sermon at church. The preacher, a man esteemed for his orthodoxy, unfolded in the ordinary manner the doctrine of the last judgment. He assumed that judgment is not executed in this world, that the wicked are successful, that the good are miserable. And then urged from reason and from scripture a compensation to be made to both parties in the next life. No offense appeared to be taken by the congregation at this doctrine as far as I could observe. When the meeting broke up, they separated without remark on the sermon. Yet what was the import of this teaching? What did the preacher mean by saying that the good are miserable in the present life? Was it that houses and lands, offices, wine, horses, dress, luxury are had by unprincipled men? Whilst the saints are poor and despised? And that a compensation is to be made to the last hereafter by giving them the like gratifications another day? Bank stock and balloons, venison and champagne. This must be the compensation intended for what else? Is it that they are to have leave to pray and praise to love and serve men? Why, that they can do now. The legitimate inference the disciple would draw was we are to have such a good time as the sinners have now or to push it to its extreme import; you sin now, we shall sin by and by. We would sin now if we could. Not being successful, we expect our revenge tomorrow. The fallacy lay in the immense concession that the bad are successful, that justice is not done now. The blindness of the preacher consisted in deferring to the base estimate of the market of what constitutes a manly success instead of confronting and convicting the world from the truth, announcing the presence of the soul, the omnipotence of the will and so establishing the standard of good and ill, of success and falsehood and summoning the dead to its present tribunal.

I find a similar base tone in the popular religious works of the day and the same doctrines assumed by the literary men when occasionally they treat the related topics. I think that our popular theology has gained in decorum and not in principle over the superstitions it has displaced, but men are better than this theology. Their daily life gives it the lie. Every ingenuous and aspiring soul leaves the doctrine behind him in his own experience and all men feel sometimes the falsehood, which they cannot demonstrate, for men are wiser than they know. That which they hear in schools and pulpits without afterthought, if said in conversation, would probably be questioned in silence. If a man dogmatized in mixed company on providence and the divine laws, he is answered by a silence that conveys well enough to an observer the dissatisfaction of the hearer, but his incapacity to make his own statement.

I shall attempt in this [essay] to record some facts that indicate the path of the law of compensation, happy beyond my expectation if I shall truly draw the smallest ark of this circle. Polarity or action and reaction we meet in every part of nature in darkness and light, in heat and cold, in the ebb and flow of waters, in male and female, in the inspiration and expiration of plants and animals, in the systole and diastole of the heart, in the undulations of fluids and of sound, in the centrifugal and centrical gravity, in electricity Galvanism and chemical affinity, super-induced magnetism at one end of a needle, the opposite magnetism takes place at the other end. If the south attracts, the north repels. To empty here, you must condense there. An inevitable dualism, bi-sex nature so that each thing is a half and suggests another thing to make it whole as spirit/matter, man/woman, subjective/objective, in/out, upper/under, motion/rest, yay/nay. Whilst the world is thus dual, so is every one of its parts. The entire system of things gets represented in every particle. There is something that resembles the ebb and flow of the sea, day and night, man and woman in a single needle of the pine, in a kernel of corn, in each individual of every animal tribe. The reaction, so grand in the elements, is repeated within these small boundaries. For example, in the animal kingdom, the physiologist has observed that no creature is our favorite, but a certain compensation balances every gift and every defect, a surplus that's given to one part is paid out of a reduction from another part of the same creature. If the head and neck are enlarged, the trunk and extremities are caught short. The theory of the mechanic forces is another example. What we gain in power is lost in time and the converse. The periodic or compensating errors of the planets is another instance. The influences of climate and soil in political history are another. The cold climate invigorates the barren soil, and does not breed fevers, crocodiles, tigers, or scorpions.

⚫ **ENTREPRENEUR TIP**

The dualism Emerson talks about here is present everywhere, even in your business. Take five minutes to jot down the ebbs and flows you have noticed in your entrepreneurial journey, or even in your day-to-day business activities. How do those ebbs and flows affect your productivity, the habits you create, and the goals you set?

The same dualism underlies the nature and condition of man. Every excess causes a defect; every defect, an excess. Every sweet has its sour. Every evil, its good. Every faculty, which is a receiver of pleasure, has an equal penalty put on its abuse. It is to answer for its moderation with its life. For every grain of wit, there is a grain of folly. For everything you have missed, you have gained something else, and for everything you gain, you lose something. If riches increase, they are increased—but use them. If a gatherer gathers too much, nature takes out of the man, which he puts into his chest, swells the estate but kills the owner. Nature hates monopolies and exceptions. The waves of the sea do not more speedily seek a level from their loftiest tossing and the varieties of condition tend to equalize themselves. There is always some leveling circumstance that puts down the overbearing, the strong, the rich, the fortunate substantially on the same ground with all others is a man too strong and fears for society and by temper and position a bad citizen, a morose ruffian with a dash of a pirate in him. Nature sends him a troop of pretty sons and daughters who were getting along in the Dames Classes at the

Village School, and love and fear for them smooths his grim scowl to courtesy. Thus, she contrives to intenerate the granite and fells bar, takes the bore out and puts the lamb in and keeps her balance true. The farmer imagines power and place are fine things, but the President has paid dear for his White House. It has commonly cost him all his peace and the best of his manly attributes to preserve for a short time so conspicuous in appearance before the world; he is content to eat dust before the real masters who stand erect behind the throne. Or do men desire the more substantial and permanent grandeur of genius? Neither has this an immunity. He, who by force of will or of thought is great and overlooks thousands; has the responsibility of overlooking with every influx of light comes new danger. Has he light? He must bear witness to the light and always outrun that sympathy which gives him such keen satisfaction. By his fidelity to new revelations of the incessant soul.

He must hate father and mother, wife and child. Has he all that the world loves and admires and covets? He must cast behind him their admiration and afflict them by fatefulness to his truth and become a byword and a hissing. This law writes the laws of the cities and nations. It will not be bought of its end in the smallest iota. It is in vain to build or plot or combine against. The things refuse to be mismanaged long. Though no checks to a new evil appear, the checks exist and will appear. If the government is cruel, the Governor's life is not safe. If you tax too high, the revenue will yield nothing. If you make the criminal code sanguinary, juries will not convict. Nothing arbitrary, nothing artificial can endure the true life and satisfactions of man seem to elude the utmost rigors or facilities of condition and to establish themselves with great indifference under all varieties of circumstance. Under all governments, the influence of character remains the same in Turkey and New England about alike under the primeval despots of Egypt; history honestly confesses that man must have been as free as culture could make him. These appearances indicate the fact that the universe is represented in every one of its particles. Everything in nature contains all the powers of nature. Everything is made of one hidden stuff as the natural it sees one type under every metamorphosis and regard a horse as a running man, a fish as a swimming man, a bird as a flying man, a tree as a rooted man. Each new form repeats not only the main character of the type but part-for-part all the details, all the aims, furtherances, hindrances, energies, and whole system of every other. Every occupation, trade, art, transaction is a compend of the world and a correlative of every other. Each one is an entire emblem of human life, of its good and ill, its trials, its enemies, its course and its end, and each one must somehow accommodate the whole man and recite all his destiny. The world globes itself in a drop of dew.

The microscope cannot find the animalcule, which is less perfect for being little. Eyes, ears, taste, smell, motion, resistance, appetite, and organs of reproduction that take hold on eternity, all find room to consist in the small creature. So do we put our life into every act. The true doctrine of omnipresence is that God reappears with all his parts in every moss and cobweb. The value of the universe contrives to throw itself into every point. If the good is there, so is the evil. If the ability, so the repulsion. If the force, so the limitation. Thus is the universe alive. All things are moral. That soul which within us is a sentiment outside of us is a law. We feel its inspirations. Out there in history we can see its fatal strength. It is almighty; all nature feels its grasp. It is in the world and the world was made by it. It is eternal but it enacts itself in time and space. Justice is not postponed. A perfect equity, a just gets balance in all parts of life. The dice of God are always loaded. The world looks like a multiplication table or a mathematical equation which, turn it how you will, balances itself. Take what figure you will, its exact value—no more, no less—still returns to you. Every secret is told, every crime is punished. Every virtue rewarded, every wrong redressed in silence and certainty. What we call retribution is the universal necessity by which the whole appears, whatever a part appears. If you see smoke, there must be fire. If you see a hand or a limb, you know that the trunk to which it belongs is there behind. Every act rewards itself or, in other words, integrates itself in a two-fold manner. First, in the thing or in real nature and secondly, in the circumstance or in the parent nature. Men call the circumstance the retribution; the casual retribution is the thing and is seen by the soul. The retribution and the circumstance is seen by the understanding. It is inseparable from the thing but is often spread over a long time and so does not become distinct until after many years. The specific strikes may follow late after the offense, but they follow because they accompany it. Crime and punishment grow out of one stem. Punishment is a fruit that unsuspectedly ripens within the flower of the pleasure which concealed it. Cause and effect, means and ends, seed and fruit cannot be severed. For the effect already blooms in the cause. The end pre-exists in the means. The fruit [is] in the seed.

Whilst dust the world will be whole and refuses to be discarded, we seek to act partially, to sunder, to appropriate. For example, to gratify the senses, we sever the pleasure of the senses from the needs of the character. The ingenuity of man has been dedicated to the solution of one problem— how to detach the sensual sweet, the sensual strong, the sensual bright, etc. from the moral sweet of the moral deep, the moral fair. That is, again, the contrived to cut clean off this upper surface so thin as to leave it bottomless. To get one end without another end. The soul says eat; the body would feast. The soul says the man and woman shall be one flesh and one soul. The body would join the flesh only. The soul says have dominion over all things to the ends of virtue. The body would have the power over things to its own ends. The soul strives a main to live and work through all things. It would be the only fact. All things shall be added unto it: power, pleasure, knowledge, beauty. The particular man aims to be somebody, to set up for himself, to tuck and haggle for a private good and in particular, to ride that he may ride, a dress that he may be dressed, to eat that he may eat and to govern that he may be seen. Men seek to be great. They would have offices, wealth, power, and fame. They think that to be great is to get only one side of nature, the sweet without the other side, the bitter. Steadily is this dividing and detaching counteracted. Up to this day it must be owned. No projector has had the smallest success. The parted water reunites behind our hand. Pleasure is taken out of pleasant things. Profit out of profitable things, power out of strong things; the moment seeks to separate them from the whole. We can no more have things and get the sensual good by itself than we can get an inside that you'll have no outside or a light without a shadow. Drive out nature with a fork. She comes running back. Life invests itself with inevitable conditions, which the unwise seek to dodge, which one and another brags that he does not know; brags that they do not touch him. But the brag is on his lips; the conditions are in his soul. If he escapes them in one part, they attack him in another more vital part. If he has escaped them in form and in the appearance, it's because he has resisted his life and fled from himself and the retribution is so much death. So signal is the favor of all attempts to make the separation of the good from the tax, that the experiment would not be tried since who trieth is to be mad, but for the circumstance that when the disease began in the will of rebellion and separation, the intellect is at once infected so that the man ceases to see God whole in each object but is able to see the sensual allurement of an object and not see the sensual hurt. He sees the mermaid's head but not the dragon's tail and thinks he can cut off that which he would have from that which he would not have. How secret art thou who dwellest in the highest heavens in silence, oh thou only great God, sprinkling with an unwearied providence certain penal blindnesses upon such as have unbridled desires. The human soul is true to these facts in the painting of fable, of history, of law, of proverbs, of conversation. It finds a tongue in literature unawares. Thus, the Greeks call Jupiter "supreme mind" but having traditionally ascribed to him many base actions, they involuntarily made amends to reason by tying up the hands of so bad a god, he is made as helpless as a King of England. Theseus knows one secret which Job must bargain for. Minerva another. He cannot get his own thunders. Minerva keeps the key of them. Of all the gods, I only know the keys that open the solid doors within whose vaults his thunders sleep. A plain confession of the inworking of the all and of its moral aim. The Indian mythology ends in the same ethics and indeed it would seem impossible for any fable to be invented and get any currency which was not moral. There is a crack in everything God has made. Always it would seem there is this vindictive circumstance dealing in at unawares even into the wild policy in which the human fancy attempted to make the bold holiday and shake itself free of the old laws.

This backstroke, this kick of the gun, certifying that the law is fatal, that in nature nothing can be given. All things are sold. This is that ancient doctrine of Nemathus, who keeps watch on the university and lets no offense go unchastised. The furies, they said, are attendance on justice and if the son in heaven should transgress his path, they would punish him. The poets related that stone walls and iron swords and leather palms had sympathy with the wrongs of their owners.

That was the belt which Ajax gave Hector that dragged the Trojan hero over the field and the wheels of the car of Achilles. And the sword which Hector gave Ajax was that on whose point Ajax fell. They recorded it when the Faizaan erected the statue to Theogenius, a victor in the games. One of his rivals went to it by night, and endeavored to throw it down by repeated blows until at least he removed it from its pedestal and was crushed to death beneath its fall.

This voice of fable has in it something divine. It came from thought above the will of the writer. That is the best part of each writer, which has nothing private in it. That is the best part of each, which he does know. That, which flowed out of his constitution and not from his two active inventions, that which in the study of a single artist, you might not easily find, but in the study of many you would abstract as the spirit of them all.

⦿ ENTREPRENEUR TIP

One point Emerson makes in this essay is that you get out of the universe what you put into it. You can experience that cause and effect when you provide guidance or mentorship to employees or up-and-coming colleagues in your industry. Think about what you can do to put out something positive into your working world. Set up a mentorship program at your company. Take a junior colleague out to lunch. Give a talk to a college business class. Put your business know-how and energy out into the world through simple, everyday acts.

We are to see that which man was tending to do in a given period and was hindered, or if you will, modified in doing by the interfering volitions of Phidias, of Dante, of Shakespeare, the organ whereby man at the moment rot. Still more striking is the expression of this fact in the proverbs of all nations, which are always the literature of reason or the statements of an absolute truth without qualifications. Proverbs, like the sacred books of each nation, are the sanctuary of the intuitions. That which the droning world chained to appearances will not allow the realist to say in his own words; it will suffer him to say in proverbs without contradiction, and this law of laws which the pulpit, the senate, and the college deny is hourly preached in all markets and all languages by flights of proverbs, whose teaching is as true and as omnipresent as that of birds and flies. All things are double one against another, tit for tat, an eye for an eye, a tooth for a tooth, blood for blood, measure for measure, love for love. Give and it shall be given to you. He that watereth shall be watered himself. What will you have, quotes God?

Pay for it and take it. Nothing ventured, nothing gained. Thou shalt be paid exactly for what thou hast done, no more, no less. Who doth not work, shall not eat. Harm watch, harm catch. Curses always recoil on the head of him who importees them. If you put a chain around the neck of a slave, the other end fastens itself around your own. Bad counsel confounds the advisor. The devil is an ass. It is thus written because it is thus in life. Our action is over mastered and characterized above our will by the law of nature. We aim at a petty end quite aside from the public good, but our act arranges itself by irresistible magnetism in align with the poles of the world. A man cannot speak, but he judges himself. With his will or against his will, he draws his portrait to the eye of his companions by every word. Every opinion reacts on him who utters it. It is a thread ball thrown at a mark but the other end remains in the thrower's bag, or rather it is a harpoon thrown at the whale unwinding as it flies a coil of cord in the boat, and if the harpoon is not good or not well thrown, it will go nigh to cut the steersman in twain or to sink the boat. You cannot do wrong without suffering wrong. No man had ever a point of pride that was not injurious to him. The exclusive and fashionable life does not see that he excludes himself from enjoyment in the attempt to appropriate it. The exclusionist in religion does not see that he shuts the door of heaven on himself in striving to shut out others. Treat men as pawns and ninepins and you shall suffer as well as they. If you leave out their heart, you shall lose your own.

⚙ ENTREPRENEUR ACTION ITEM
Make Time for Mentorship

In "Compensation," Emerson meditates on the idea that what we put into the universe, we get back. In other words, there is a dualism that creates balance in the world. This is nowhere truer than in the universe of entrepreneurship. You will get out of your journey exactly what you put into it. One great example of this can be found in networking and mentorship, particularly in highly focused mastermind groups. Being an entrepreneur is a busy job. But if you can take time out to connect with other like-minded business owners in a mastermind setting, you can not only share your expertise, but also get some in return. That said, when you're the boss, it can be near impossible to escape from the office to connect with other entrepreneurs for more than an hour or two. But the less you can afford the time, the more you need it. Here are six reasons why:

1. Perspective

Distancing yourself from the daily grind provides an entirely new view on your business—and your life. Your shoulders sink a little bit from their usual position near your ears. Those email messages waiting in your inbox seem a little less urgent than they did 24 hours ago. Just as objects in the rearview mirror are closer than they appear, problems seen from inside the office appear larger than they actually are.

2. Resource Sharing

In our world of information overload, it's impossible to be up to date on everything. Swapping resources—whether the latest trend in project management or the name of a great app developer—is one of the most valuable parts of connecting with other business owners. Come with your recommendations as well as your wish list and leave with your desires fulfilled.

3. Breathing Room

The poet Khalil Gibran wrote that to experience a successful romantic relationship, couples should " . . . let there be spaces in your togetherness." This is great advice for business relationships, too. Retreating gives your employees a chance to sink or swim without your immediate guidance, and there's no better cure for a control freak than to watch (from a distance) as the business not just survives, but thrives in your absence.

4. The Power of the Collective Mind

"No two minds ever come together without thereby creating a third, invisible, intangible force, which may be likened to a third mind [the master mind]," wrote Napoleon Hill. Anyone who's ever been part of a serious mastermind group can attest to this "third mind" force. Throw out a business problem, then sit and listen while your colleagues go to work dismantling your obstacle and suggesting a plethora of ideas, most of which would never have occurred to any individual.

5. Focus

On any given day, 101 possible projects clamor for your attention, and that list gets even longer when you're out of the office. Whether you're away for a day or a weekend, having a specific intention will give your retreat structure and purpose. By setting a narrow target, you can filter out all the possible distractions and laser in on what's most important to tackle right now.

6. Connections

While it's great to head out to dinner with a colleague, you don't really get to know someone until you see them at 7 a.m. on their way to the shower, at lunch after a full morning struggling with a new customer service standard operating procedure (SOP), and after a long night of karaoke. After spending extended time with your mastermind partners, you'll love them or hate the very sound of their breathing. You'll either end up great friends, or you'll thank your lucky stars you never signed that multi-year partnership agreement. Nothing serves as a better crucible than a few days in close quarters.

There is no telling what incredible synergistic results you might achieve from spending a few days with your mastermind group. From new relationships to new product ideas to new inspiration, a mastermind retreat can give you support, renewal, and even a good kick in the pants. Get unplugged and give yourself a chance to really master your business—with the help of your mastermind.

CHAPTER FOUR

Selling

Paul Harvey

Paul Harvey was a famous talk-radio broadcaster, and his program, "The Rest of the Story," was popular worldwide. He was a radio broadcaster for over seventy years and was well known for his plain talks.

At one time, his broadcasts on ABC were carried on 1,200 radio stations, 400 Armed Forces networks, and in 300 newspapers. Harvey's broadcasts reached over 24 million people.

"The Rest of the Story" was presented as little-known or forgotten facts pertaining to a well-known news story at the time. The broadcasts were always concluded with a variation of the tagline "and now you know the rest of the story."

This chapter features Harvey's speech on "Selling." It was originally presented in 1976, 200 years after the signing of the Declaration of Independence. You will notice the examples he references were appropriate for the times, so feel free to think of your own examples that may be relevant to our current business and geopolitical climate.

⊛ ⊛ ⊛

WE ARE ALL IN SALES

Everybody is a salesman. If you compare occupations to sports, selling is most like football in the commission selling of a quality product. Boy, that's pro football in the big leagues.

Selling is a profession that combines all the psychology of a quarterback with the calculated risk of slam-bang, head-on, hit-the-line body contact. No profession more than selling demands a person to pick themselves up, dust themselves off, and keep on keeping on; and few rewards are more thrilling than a signed dotted line. And the fiercer the competition, the more precious the prize.

You know what I think? I recently instituted a new series of programs on the ABC network called "The Rest of The Story" because I think there is no more thrilling adventure story in the literature of commerce than the several Horatio Alger stories of those who learned the skill of overcoming resistance with persistence when selling. Richard Sears was a mail order watch salesman when he and Albert Roebuck teamed up. Billy Graham was a Fuller brush man. William Wrigley peddled products door-to-door, and others who got their first training in patience and perseverance by selling face-to-face were Abraham Lincoln, and Gary Cooper, and George Peabody, and Arthur Godfrey.

To me, there's no more inspiring story anywhere in American literature than the story of James "Cash" Penney. Remember, at an age that most men expected to retire, Mr. Penney started over. He was flat broke. He was $7 million in debt. He was a frail, nervous, and physical wreck and had been committed to a sanitarium. His fortune gone and his health broken, Jim Penney, at 56, began a comeback until healthy, happy, and 90, he headed an advanced empire of almost 2,000 J.C. Penney stores. And Horatio Alger still lives.

Rich DeVos and Jay Van Andel started in the basement of Jay's modest home in Michigan 18 years ago, and since then they've developed a selling organization which has 250,000 distributors [you know it as Amway]. No profession has done more to raise our level of living by raising our level of *longing*. And you don't learn selling in school. The only two universities, as far as I know, that offer a degree in this high-paying profession are Memphis State and Syracuse.

But when you learn to sell yourself and your product, the horizon is limitless. Half the presidents of America's top 500 corporations came up through sales and/or marketing.

But now, football and selling take guts. The other guy doesn't get out of your way; he purposely does everything he can to get *in* your way. And for most of us, there's no guaranteed security, no protracted vacations, no promise of early retirement, but—man alive—who would want to retire from a vocation that's more fun than most any avocation could be?

I am a salesman and will be until the day they nail the lid on that box. As a matter of fact, shortly after they nail the lid on that box, I'm likely really to have to be doing some selling. But I'm ready for it. When St. Peter says, "Paul Harvey, what'd you do down there that makes you think you deserve to be up here?" I'm going to say, "Sir, I don't deserve to be here, but I had your promise that believing in certain things, I'll get here, so I'm here. And just this much more—just this much more, St. Peter, down there on that ball of mud, planet Earth, there is a potential paradise called the United States of America, the world's finest government under God. Sir, I did what I could while I could to keep it sold on itself."

SELLING THE IDEA OF AMERICA

Nowhere else do people criticize their leaders as they do in our country. Do you know if any man dared to talk about your wife in a nitpicking, carping, unflattering, sometimes cruel way the way some people talk about your president, you'd punch him in the mouth? Turn that around, and hang our flag right side up again, and you'll have Americans standing and saluting, and cheering again, and believing again in our country and in themselves. Honesty and integrity could become as fashionable as shortcutting now is. Even work could have a new dignity and a new desirability when we're working for something that's bigger than ourselves.

Now every man and woman [reading this] is in the front lines of a high noon defense of what's left of freedom. At whatever job, however lofty, tomorrow morning you're going to be selling yourself or your service or your product. Will you please help to resell our country to our countrymen before we all end up with 15 percent of nothing?

I don't think any president, for all his bicentennial years' speeches, for all the inaugural pageantry, pointing the way to a reaffirmation of Americanism, I don't think any president, doing the best he can do, can match you when it comes to showing the way, nurturing the deep roots of this fragile American beauty rose, fertilizing it with shoe leather, and watering it with sweat. American capitalism is no longer viable, unless you reprove its virility every day.

❧ ENTREPRENEUR TIP

Harvey mentions many of the social and political issues of his time in this selection, and how they can affect everyday business practices. It's always a good idea to keep abreast of the national issues that may affect your own business, even if you don't consider yourself a history buff. Getting to know the history of your industry and its place in your country's story can help you chart trends over time and identify issues that may affect your bottom line.

There's a recession in Raleigh, North Carolina. Every day, Mike Sills sells himself in Raleigh, North Carolina, washing cars wherever. He's got himself a van loaded with 55-gallon barrels of water and detergent. He makes house calls to wash your car wherever it's parked. He has wax if you like, and he always vacuums the interior at no extra charge. In Savannah,

Illinois, the Savannah Army depot closed down. Unemployment went to 12 percent of the local population, but in Savannah, Illinois, Mr. Martin Blasix is self-employed. Every morning at daybreak, he's down on the bank of the Plum River spading worms and selling them to fishermen and bait shops. He digs usually 600 every day and sells them at 60 worms to the dollar. He puts a sign out front: Worms for Sale. Incidentally, Mr. Blasix says these are good times for his business when people have time to fish, but are still too lazy to dig.

Selling to Skeptics

Did you know that the Union Bank of Switzerland sent it's emissaries all over the world looking for the best place to live? They went all over the world, went back to Switzerland and fed their findings into a computer, all their statistics, asked the computer where in the world is the best place to live, and guess where? You're there! Everywhere else on planet Earth, you would have to work more hours to buy food, clothing, and rent. So while Americans' standard of living is still the best in this world, I see a survey which says that a third of voting-age Americans, one third of us, believe that our nation is over the hill. I guess they are judging from what they see, hear, and read. They figure our future is now in the past, and from here on, it's all downhill. Now, wouldn't that rot your socks!

In this country, we don't plow up the garden just because some weeds sprout in it, and if we'd leave it, if we'd give up and run for cover every time it rained, we'd still just be 13 colonies. Do you realize that in spite of the worst, we've been able to do all right? Our Americanism is made of very durable stuff.

In the 200 years since we've weaned ourselves, every other nation on Earth has been turned upside down. Two hundred years ago, England and France were monarchies; kings ruled both of them. Italy and Germany weren't even on the map. They didn't even exist. Our Latin American neighbors were colonies. China was ruled by the Manchu, Japan by the shoguns. It was only what we built here that's done so well, and it's remained more or less intact. But it was for us, our generation, recently to become distressed with some of these problems that I've outlined in which some of our temporarily elected leaders failed us, and some decided to burn our flag. Oh for goodness sake, our flag has failed us in no way. However, many of us have sometimes failed it.

There are very real problems deserving of our urgent consideration; Uncle Sam is sick. But what I'm saying is, Uncle Sam's been sick before. Every few years he gets sick. And every now and then in November, sometimes in between, he falls down and he gets up, and he gets going again.

You know, I had a birthday last September and you want to hear about a sobering experience! I awakened that September morn on a Missouri farm to the sudden realization that a boy baby born when I was born in Tulsa, Oklahoma, had a life expectancy of 50 years and six months. Suddenly, I am on borrowed time. And that's not the worst of it. The distress is real when I say this next, but it's haunted me ever since.

I realized that morning that I, Paul Harvey, was now one-fourth as old as our country. My goodness, I had always thought of my beloved Republic as having such deep roots. Our country is only four times as old as I am, for goodness sake. Our country is not over the hill; it's barely a beardless, post-puberty adolescent. What's messing up our country is not senility, it's acne. (I'm not far from the finish, so stay with me.) Our balance of trade with other nations is unbalanced in their favor. For the ninth straight month, mostly because of the higher prices, we're having to pay for all that imported oil, and the OPEC nations are in conference right now getting ready to tack on another 10 percent. Another penny a gallon for gasoline, another four cents a gallon for crude. I'm going to say this next with due deference to those who are inconvenienced or hurt by it, but I think in my third of a century as a professional parade watcher, this so-called energy crisis might be the best thing that's happened to our America the Beautiful to get our people off their posteriors and back to using their imaginations again. Boy, what exciting years these next ten are going to be! So if they're going to charge us too much for oil, we'll use something else. Off Florida, we're going to sink turbines in the Gulf and we might be able to harness a movement of water greater than 10,000 Niagaras. We do what we have to do. Off the rock-bound coast of Maine, we may be able to harness the tides to produce commercial quantities of mechanical or electrical power. In far-western states, we'll generate increasing amounts of electricity with geothermal steam. Solar energy. We'll see the second coming of age for nuclear energy, already producing 11 percent of our nation's electricity. And in the name of progress, we're going to harness the wind with streamlined, sophisticated windmills.

Necessity (and Recessions) Breeds Invention

Recessions teach resourcefulness. For example, Economy Furniture Company in Austin, Texas, a furniture company now, is generating electricity for operating its machinery by burning sawdust that they used to throw away.

> ● ENTREPRENEUR TIP
>
> Looking for a recession-proof business? Many experts point to franchises as safer bets to weather financial storms. Look for businesses that provide essential or critical services or staple items that never go out of style.

Pioneer Hybrid in Marengo, Iowa, is now drying its seed corn with an exotic fuel. Guess what it is. No, not solar energy. Not nuclear energy. Hybrid corn is now being dried by burning corn cobs.

Now why didn't we think of that a long time ago? Because oil was $2 a barrel and we didn't have to. Now oil's going to be $11, $12, $13 dollars a barrel, and these alternative energies begin to make sense. And there's a downtown office building in suburban Milwaukee, West Allis, which is entirely heated and cooled without any gas, without any oil, electricity, or solar energy—by harnessing the body heat of its 7,000 occupants. And Americans, Lord willing, you and I are going to be together someday a decade from now talking about sources of energy we are using in our everyday living which I can't tell you about yet because the words for it aren't in the dictionary yet. So soon, we will forget the petroleum industry that made us the powerhouse of this planet, which was born before the turn of another century, and all because there was a fuel shortage. There was a fuel shortage so acute in the 1860s that a Boston newspaper headlined "The Lights Will Go Out All Over the World" because of a shortage of whale oil. That's why we started punching holes in Texas. We were running out of blubber.

Now running low on petroleum, we just might even rediscover the value of elbow grease. Oh, my dear Americans who are the energetic minority, and confidentially, we always were, are on the threshold of the greatest national social, political, and economic rearrangement in a hundred years, and because there are so many goof-offs, there has never been so much room at the top.

You know, this is going to be rough on us reactionaries these next ten years. But if we can somehow keep our intellectual arteries sufficiently pliable to accept and adapt to inevitable change, oh, what a time to be alive.

SELLING OPTIMISM

And now the last thing that I'd like for you to remember is something that ought to reinforce your PMA. Every optimist in history has been right. And every pessimist in history is buried in an unmarked grave.

You know of all the times when man could live there is no more perfect one, no more exciting one, than this. This is really a very rare moment in the history of the world. In our own country, the smoke shrouding Capitol Hill has been ventilated and our economy is back in high gear; by all standards 1977 will be a very green year. Environmental pollution, air and water, everywhere that it's measured is measurably less. On campuses, admission deans everywhere tell me that now the preoccupation, even in the freshman and sophomore years, is with vocational education.

Historians will not find many of our any 200 years when we have enjoyed less social ferment, fewer labor strikes, less disease, and more take-home prosperity. Even the crime fever, at least you would agree, is subsiding.

At year end, 1976 has shown an unprecedented investment, public and private, in developing inexhaustible supplies of clean air; music is almost singable again; uppers and downers are a fading fad and the comb is making a comeback.

On the doorstep of 1977, our nation's most underappreciated minority, our farmers, are about to move up. Dollar shrinkage is some less than last year and much less than anywhere else. Americans have led the world in exploration of other worlds, and if we've not found life there, the fallout from our adventuring has contributed so much to a better life here. And the horizons for women have been pushed back beyond the kitchen window. A rather long way beyond.

Physically, our sons and daughters are now so improved over any heretofore that we can't reprint the record books fast enough to catch up with our taller, healthier, faster, stronger athletes, and there has been no other time nor other place where builders and manufacturers and merchants and advertisers have been in such vigorous competition with one another and with themselves to provide for you some things better, better tasting, better for you, longer lasting, or more beautiful. And with all the bounty and the beauty that would surely lull us to sleep, we're still just enough blessed with some unsolved problems and inspiring challenges to keep us awake. So it's little wonder that ours is the only land where people are standing in line trying to get in instead of dying trying to get out.

And you in the front lines of this new economic renaissance, you of all people are right where the action is. Boy, what a thrilling time this is to be an American. You know, of all the recent bumper stickers, the one I like best says, "America—she ain't perfect, but we ain't done yet."

SELLING SELF-DISCIPLINE

We cannot herald this land of the free without at least some apology, when you know you can't go out to the airport and get on an airliner without submitting yourself and your luggage and even your underwear to search. Not because there's tyranny in government, but because there's anarchy in the unbuttoned brains of a handful who don't deserve to be free so the rest of us can't be. That's why I say self-government without self-discipline won't work.

And you who bristle about the alphabetical agencies that usurp your prerogatives, let's imagine that there were no Food and Drug Administration. Let's just imagine that starting tomorrow there is no FDA, then how many roaches will be the allowable limit in your bottle of ketchup? Come on now, how much would be too many bug droppings in your oatmeal? And would you without government supervision market lethal blowguns as Christmas toys? Self-government without self-discipline won't work.

The National Advertising Review Board is trying self-regulation, trying to police advertising claims so that government won't have to, and just this week it told Alpo, *Please stop implying that your pet food product is all meat when it's not.* You and I can remember in the old pre-regulated days when the insurance salesman said anything to get his foot in the door and promised anything to get a customer commitment. And the FTC is probing some practices of which we cannot be proud. How safe would coal miners be without governmental scrutiny? So the number of government regulatory agencies has doubled in ten years.

A few misused freedoms and we're all that much less free. But self-government without self-discipline won't work. A New York manufacturer will lock his fire doors and boaters will make toilets of beaches. But now you know what? We're fishing in the Great Lakes again. And the Cuyahoga River in Ohio does not catch fire anymore. And the air is measurably cleaner.

All I said that you might possibly have missed was that self-government without self-discipline won't work. We are making measurable, provable progress in cleaning up our air and cleaning up our water, but what a shame that government had to do it. Yet the more responsibility we vacate, the more government will move in and free enterprise will be that much less free.

Did it ever occur to you that the Declaration of Independence about which we've been making such a fuss this bicentennial year also included an important declaration of dependence also? I'm not sure that the declaration of dependence is not even of transcendent importance. It's in the next-to-last paragraph where the founders of our nation called upon the guidance and blessing of almighty God.

Now, Paul Harvey, you've gone from commentating and started preaching. And I don't mean to, but faith is a responsibility infinitively higher than any to which I would aspire, but I can't separate goodness and badness from today's news and explain it because every ugly headline on page one is because somebody's emotions got out of whack. He might have been smarter than all get out, smart enough to be an atomic scientist or a professor, bank official, but if he was emotionally colorblind, don't you see, he was an unguided missile inevitably destined to self-destruct.

Self-government without self-discipline won't work. Now, on the sunshine side of the ledger, there is not one of these problems which bedevil us today which wouldn't respond but to a formula as simple as do unto others.

I mean all of them. Crime, pollution, inflation, every one of them. We don't need more laws, piled on laws, seeking salvation by legislation. All we got to do is revert to obedience to the basic ten. Said another way, we have to resell our home folks on the foundation stone of our Americanism.

⚬ ENTREPRENEUR ACTION ITEM
Using Sales Secrets to Position Yourself as an Expert

In "Selling," Paul Harvey uses the American experiment as a basis for his lessons on the nature of selling. Whether you are selling a concept, an experience, or an experiment, it's all about positioning yourself as a trustworthy expert. That's especially true if your product, idea, or concept is traditionally considered a "tough sell," like the concept of self-discipline he writes about above.

If, as Harvey posits, everyone is a salesperson at heart, then we all must have the same approach, right? Not so fast. Your sales approach (and what you're selling) depends largely on your goals. And if you feel confident and knowledgeable about the product, service, or idea you're selling, then you are well positioned to not only sell it, but yourself as well. The most successful salespeople in the world don't come across as salespeople. Instead, they carry themselves as experts in their industry who can solve key challenges for their ideal prospects. Simply put, if you're in the business of selling, then you're an expert in whatever you sell. It's up to you to make sure your prospects know it. While your prospects only see what's going on at their own companies, you can offer them a valuable bird's eye view of trends across the entire industry. But do your customers see it that way? If not, it's because you're coming off as salesy instead of as an expert.

The following eight simple keys will help you build a reputation as an expert in whatever you sell, so you can earn prospects' trust and start to achieve your sales goals.

Don't Think Like a Salesperson

If you want to come across as an expert to your prospects, you must first stop being "salesy." That means you have to stop thinking like a salesperson. When you think like a salesperson, you jump at any chance to pitch your product or service. Instead, slow down and listen. Strive to identify if your prospects are a fit in the first place. Practicing thoughtful intentionality is the first step toward being viewed as an expert in the eyes of your customers.

Adopt a Doctor's Mindset

Instead of thinking like a salesperson, try adopting the mindset of a doctor. I've never met a doctor who used a pitch like, "We have this incredible new procedure that I just can't wait to tell you about! It's going to change everything!" Rather, good doctors ask questions to make sure they understand your pain before making a diagnosis. Mimic this approach by making it your goal to understand your prospects' deepest frustrations before you propose a solution.

Lose the P.E.P.

Most salespeople are full of P.E.P.—persuasion, enthusiasm, and pitching. They've been told this is the key to closing more sales, but it isn't true. If you have to persuade a prospect, then they probably aren't a good fit for what you sell. Enthusiasm comes off as salesy and insincere, and pitching is the opposite of trying to understand a prospect's problem. Instead of turning your sales meeting into a P.E.P. rally, adopt a genuine approach to understand and diagnose key challenges. When you do, prospects will view you as an expert they can trust.

Share Challenges You've Observed

As an expert, you have valuable industry information that your prospects would love to know. Capture their attention and increase your perceived value by sharing some of that information at the start of your conversations with prospects. Try listing a few examples of challenges you've seen in their industry. This will provide value, give the prospect something to relate to, and serve as a launching pad for a great discussion.

Ask About Their Challenges

Once you've shared a few common challenges you've observed, simply ask, "Do any of these challenges ring true to you?" Simple questions like this create more value when you sell, in addition to engaging prospects and encouraging them to open up to you. If you can get someone to articulate a challenge that they've yet to share with anyone else, you'll immediately gain respect as an authority in your field who can tap into, and ultimately resolve, big problems.

Know When to Walk Away

What do you do if you ask, "Do any of these challenges ring true to you?" and your prospect answers, "no?" Well, if a prospect doesn't have challenges you can solve, then it's probably not a good fit. When this happens, you must be willing to disqualify. Walk away without looking back so you can spend your time with qualified prospects instead. Customers will respect and trust you more when they notice you aren't trying to push a product they don't need.

Remember the 15 Percent Rule

Salespeople should never talk for more than 15 percent of a meeting. Talking doesn't put you in control of a conversation—great questions do. Engaged body language, thoughtful questions, and small prompts such as, "Really?" are all great tools to keep the customer talking. Follow this rule, and prospects will view you as a thoughtful listener and an expert.

Never Need a Sale

In all fairness, there may be times when you really do need a sale to pay your bills, but prospects should never be able to tell. When you come across as successful and confident, prospects will believe you don't need their business. Instead, you're simply meeting with them because you think your offering will truly help them. Relaxed confidence is attractive to prospects, and an air of success will suggest that you're an established expert in your field.

You're already an expert in your industry. Now it's time to act like one. Which of these keys will you use to establish yourself as an expert in the eyes of your prospect?

CHAPTER FIVE

The Story of the Other Wise Man

Henry Van Dyke

Henry Van Dyke held several occupations during his life, including educator, clergyman, and writer. One of his best-known publications is the story of "The Story of the Other Wise Man," a short novel about the wise man who also saw the star rising in Bethlehem, and set out to follow it, yet did not arrive with the other wise men.

Following is an abridged version of this parable. The main idea in the novel is about finding solutions to problems. If you have accomplished many things, but still have not reached a major goal, this story is for you. At heart, this story is a business parable, designed to walk the reader through the journey of success with all the fits and starts, triumphs and tragedies that remind us we are more than our work. And sometimes, our end goals aren't really destinations, but rather, catalysts for finding who we really are.

◈ ◈ ◈

A CLASSIC TALE WITH A TWIST

You know the story of the Three Wise Men of the East and how they traveled from far away to offer their gifts at the manger-cradle in Bethlehem. But have you ever heard the story of the Other Wise Man, who also saw the star in its rising and set out to follow it, yet did not arrive with his brethren in the presence of the young child Jesus? Of the great desire of this fourth pilgrim, and how it was denied, yet accomplished in the denial? Of his many wanderings and the probing of his soul? Of the long way of his seeking, and the strange way of his finding, the one whom he sought?

In the days when Augustus Caesar was master of many kings and Herod reigned in Jerusalem, there lived in the city of Ecbatana, among the mountains of Persia, a certain man named Artaban, the Magi. Artaban was holding council with his friends. He stood by the doorway to greet his guests, a tall, dark man of about 40 years, with brilliant eyes set near together under his broad brow, and firm lines graven around his thin, fine lips.

"Welcome!" he said, in his low, pleasant voice, as one after another entered the room.

There were nine visitors, differing widely in age but alike in the richness of their dress of many-colored silks, and in the massive golden collars around their necks, marking them as Parthian nobles, and in the winged circles of gold resting upon their breasts, the sign of the followers of Zoroaster.

"You have come tonight," said Artaban, looking around the circle of nine men, "at my call, as the faithful scholars of Zoroaster, to renew your worship and rekindle your faith in the God of Purity, even as His fire has been rekindled on the altar. We worship not the fire, but Him of whom it is the chosen symbol, because it is the purest of all created things. It speaks to us of one who is Light and Truth. Hear me, then, my friends," said Artaban, "while I tell you of a new light and truth that have come to me through the most ancient of all signs. I have kept this prophecy in the secret place of my soul."

He drew from the breast of his tunic two small rolls of fine parchment with writing upon them, and unfolding them carefully, set them upon his knee. "They have been shown to me and to three of my companions among the Magi: Caspar, Melchior, and Balthazar. We have searched the ancient tablets of Chaldea and computed the time. It falls in this year. We have studied the sky, and in the spring of the year, we saw two of the greatest stars draw near together in the sign of the Fish, which is the house of the Hebrews. We also saw a new star there, which shone for one night and then vanished. If the star shines again, they will wait ten days for me at the temple, and then we will set out together for Jerusalem, to see and worship the promised one who shall be born King of Israel. I believe the sign will come. I have made ready for the journey. I have sold my possessions and bought these three jewels—a sapphire, a ruby, and a pearl—to carry them as tribute to the King. And I ask you to go with me on the pilgrimage, that we may have joy together in finding the Prince who is worthy to be served."

While he was speaking, he thrust his hand into the inmost fold of his girdle and drew out three great gems: one blue as a fragment of the night sky, one redder than a ray of sunrise, and one as pure as the peak of a snow mountain at twilight—and laid them on the outspread scrolls before him.

But his friends looked on with strange and alien eyes. A veil of doubt and mistrust came over their faces, like a fog creeping up from the marshes to hide the hills. They glanced at each other with looks of wonder and pity, as those who have listened to incredible sayings, the story of a wild vision, or the proposal of an impossible enterprise.

At last, one of them said, "Artaban, this is a vain dream. It comes from too much looking upon the stars and the cherishing of lofty thoughts."

So one by one, the nine men left the house of Artaban, and he was left in solitude.

He gathered up the jewels and replaced them in his girdle. For a long time, he stood and watched the flame that flickered and sank upon the altar. Then he crossed the hall, lifted the heavy curtain, and passed out between the pillars of porphyry to the terrace of the roof.

All night long, Vasda, the swiftest of Artaban's horses, had been waiting, saddled and bridled in her stall, pawing the ground impatiently and shaking her bit as if she shared the eagerness of her master's purpose, though she knew not its meaning.

Before the birds had fully roused to their strong, high, joyful chant of morning song, before the white mist had begun to lift lazily from the plain, the other wise man was in the saddle, riding swiftly along the high road which skirted the base of Mount Orontes, westward.

Artaban pressed onward until he arrived at nightfall of the tenth day, beneath the shattered walls of populous Babylon. A grove of date palms made an island of gloom in the pale yellow field. As she passed into the shadow, Vasda slackened her pace and began to pick her way more carefully. Near the farther end of the darkness, an excess of caution seemed to fall upon her.

She felt her steps before her delicately, carrying her head low and sighing now and then with apprehension. At last, she gave a quick breath of anxiety and dismay and stood stock still, quivering in every muscle, before a dark object in the shadow of the last palm tree.

Artaban dismounted. The dim starlight revealed the form of a man lying across the road. His humble dress and the outline of his haggard face showed that he was probably one of the laborers who still dwelt in great numbers around the city. His pallid skin, dry and yellow as parchment, bore the mark of the deadly fever which ravaged the marshlands in autumn. The chill of death was in his lean hand, and as Artaban released it, the arm fell back inertly upon the motionless breast.

He turned away with a thought of pity, leaving the body to that strange burial which the Magis deem most fitting: the funeral of the desert. But as he turned, a long, faint, ghostly sigh came from the man's lips. The bony fingers gripped the hem of his robe and held him fast. Artaban's heart leaped to his throat, not with fear but with a dumb resentment at the importunity of this blind delay. His spirit throbbed and fluttered with the urgency of the crisis. Should he risk the great reward of his faith for the sake of a single deed of charity? Should he turn aside, if only for a moment, from the following of the star, to give a cup of cold water to a poor, perishing man?

He turned back to the sick man. Loosening the grasp of his hand, he carried him to a little mound at the foot of the palm tree. He unbound the thick folds of the turban and opened the garment above the sunken breast. He brought water from one of the small canals nearby and moistened the sufferer's brow and mouth. They spoke quiet introductions as Artaban told the man he could rest and heal, then perhaps find shelter nearby. The man raised his trembling hand solemnly to Heaven and asked a blessing on Artaban in his travels.

Riding on, Artaban could find no sign of his friends. He finally arrived at the edge of a terrace, where he saw a little cairn of broken bricks, and under them, a piece of papyrus that read, "We have waited past the midnight and can delay no longer."

Artaban sat down upon the ground and covered his head in despair. "How can I cross the desert," said he, "with no food and with a spent horse? I must return to Babylon, sell my sapphire and buy a train of camels and provisions for the journey. I may never overtake my friends. Only God, the merciful, knows whether I shall lose the sight of the King, because I tarried to show mercy."

Artaban moved steadily onward until he arrived at Bethlehem. The other wise men had already been there and had laid their gifts of gold and frankincense and myrrh.

The streets of the village seemed deserted, and Artaban wondered whether the men had all gone up to the hill-pastures to bring down their sheep. From the open door of a cottage, he heard the sound of a woman's voice, singing softly. He entered and found a young mother, hushing her baby to rest. She told him of the strangers from the Far East who had appeared in the village three days ago, and how they said that a star had guided them to the place where Joseph of Nazareth was lodging with his wife and her newborn child, and how they had paid reverence to the child and given him many rich gifts.

"But the travelers disappeared again," she continued, "as suddenly as they had come. We were afraid at the strangeness of their visit. We could not understand it. The man of Nazareth took the child and his mother and fled away that same night, secretly, and it was whispered that they were going to Egypt. Ever since, there has been a spell upon the village; something evil hangs over it. They say that the Roman soldiers are coming from Jerusalem to force a new tax from us, and the men have driven the flocks and herds far back among the hills and hidden themselves to escape it."

Suddenly, there came the noise of a wild confusion in the streets of the village, a shrieking and wailing of women's voices, a clangor of brazen trumpets and a clashing of swords, and a desperate cry: "The soldiers! The soldiers of Herod! They are killing our children."

The young mother's face grew white with terror. She clasped her child to her bosom and crouched, motionless, in the darkest corner of the room, covering him with the folds of her robe lest he should wake and cry.

But Artaban went quickly and stood in the doorway of the house. His broad shoulders filled the portal from side to side and the peak of his white cap all but touched the lintel.

The soldiers came hurrying down the street with bloody hands and dripping swords. At the sight of the stranger in his imposing dress, they hesitated with surprise. The captain of the band approached the threshold to thrust him aside, but Artaban did not stir. His face was as calm as though he were watching the stars, and in his eyes there burned that steady radiance before which even the half-tamed hunting leopard shrinks and then pauses in his leap. He held the soldier silently for an instant and then said in a low voice, "I am all alone in this place, and I am waiting to give this jewel to the prudent captain who will leave me in peace."

He showed the ruby, glistening in the hollow of his hand like a great drop of blood.

The captain was amazed at the splendor of the gem. The pupils of his eyes expanded with desire, and the hard lines of greed wrinkled around his lips. He stretched out his hand and took the ruby.

"March on!" he cried to his men. "There is no child here. The house is empty."

The clamor and the clang of arms passed down the street, as the headlong fury of the chase sweeps by the secret covert where the trembling deer is hidden. Artaban re-entered the cottage. He turned his face to the east and prayed, "God of truth, forgive my sin. I have said the thing that is not, to save the life of a child, and two of my gifts are gone. I have spent for man that which was meant for God. Shall I ever be worthy to see the face of the King?"

But the voice of the woman weeping for joy in the shadow behind him said very gently, "Because thou hast saved the life of my little one, may the Lord bless thee and keep thee; the Lord make His face to shine upon thee and be gracious unto thee; the Lord lift up His countenance upon thee and give thee peace."

In my mind's eyes, I imagined Artaban's journeys. I saw him moving among the throngs of men in populous Egypt. I saw him again at the foot of the pyramids. I saw him again in an obscure house of Alexandria, taking counsel with a Hebrew rabbi, saying, "And remember, my son," said he, fixing his eyes upon the face of Artaban, "the King whom thou seekest is not to be found in a palace, nor among the rich and powerful. Those who seek Him will do well to look among the poor and the lowly, the sorrowful and the oppressed."

So I saw the other wise man again and again. He passed through countries where famine lay heavy upon the land and the poor were crying for bread. He made his dwelling in plague-stricken cities, where the sick were languishing in the bitter companionship of helpless misery. He visited the oppressed and the afflicted in the gloom of subterranean prisons, and the crowded wretchedness of slave markets, and the weary toil of galley ships. In all this populous and intricate world of anguish, though he found none to worship, he found many to help. He fed the hungry and clothed the naked and healed the sick and comforted the captive. And his years passed more swiftly than the weaver's shuttle that flashes back and forth through the loom, while the web grows and the invisible pattern is completed.

It seemed almost as if he had forgotten his quest. But once, I saw him for a moment as he stood alone at sunrise, waiting at the gate of a Roman prison. He had taken from a secret resting place in his bosom a pearl, the last of his jewels. As he looked at it, a mellower luster, a soft and iridescent light, full of shifting gleams of azure and rose, trembled upon its surface. Three-and-thirty years of the life of Artaban had passed away since he began his journey, and he was still a pilgrim and a seeker after light. His hair, once darker than the cliffs of Zagros, was now white as the wintry snow that covered them. His eyes that once flashed like flames of fire were dull as embers, smoldering among the ashes.

Worn and weary and ready to die, but still looking for the King, he had come for the last time to Jerusalem. He had often visited the holy city before and had searched through all its lanes, crowded hovels, and prisons, without finding any trace of the family of Nazarenes who had fled from Bethlehem long ago. But now, it seemed as if he must make one more effort, and something whispered in his heart that at last, he might succeed.

It was the season of the Passover. But on this day, a singular agitation was visible in the multitude. The sky was veiled with a portentous gloom. Currents of excitement seemed to flash through the crowd. A secret tide was sweeping them all one way. The clatter of sandals and the soft, thick sound of thousands of bare feet shuffling over the stones flowed unceasingly along the street that leads to the Damascus gate.

Artaban joined a group of people and inquired of them the cause of the tumult and where they were going. They replied that they were going to Golgotha to witness an execution. [What the author is referring to here is, of course, the story of the crucifixion.]

So the old man followed the multitude with slow and painful steps toward the Damascus gate of the city. Just beyond the entrance of the guardhouse, a troop of Macedonian soldiers came down the street, dragging a young girl with torn dress and disheveled hair. As the Magi paused to look at her with compassion, she broke suddenly from the hands of her tormentors and threw herself at his feet, clasping him around the knees, asking him for pity and mercy.

Artaban trembled. It was the old conflict in his soul, which had come to him in the palm grove of Babylon and in the cottage at Bethlehem: the conflict between the expectation of faith and the impulse of love.

Was it his great opportunity, or his last temptation? He could not tell. One thing only was clear in the darkness of his mind: It was inevitable. [He knew he must help the woman by giving her his last jewel, a pearl. And in doing so, he realized that his journey was the gift all along, and in giving to those less fortunate, he had realized the power of charity and the gift of selflessness. He had given himself to others, reaping the greatest reward.]

⚜ ENTREPRENEUR ACTION ITEM

What Smart Entrepreneurs Know About Problem-Solving

Just like in the parable you just read, problems in the real world (especially in the world of entrepreneurship) can often be opportunities in disguise. Artaban thought he was going on an endless, fruitless journey. But it turns out, the problems he faced along the way were really opportunities to grow—not obstacles to overcome. The gifts of the self are best when shared, as he learned after sharing his riches with those less fortunate. And in that sharing of the self, Artaban found that what you are looking for is often right in front of you. But as Artaban also wondered, who are we solving the problems for? Ourselves? Others? In terms of business, is it for our employees? Who is the solution really for in the long run?

Whether you're developing an innovative product that will take the world by storm or solving a payroll problem that's taking up way too much of your time, your business needs creative problem-solving. Every day. While Archimedes and Newton had world-changing epiphanies that simply dawned on them, the rest of us mere mortals could use some help in this department.

This rings even truer in our rapidly evolving economy. Established business models are stumbling to find their way as slick new formats give the old hands a run for their money. So how do the best in the business rise above and stay ahead, day after day? Here are some insights.

Two Heads Are Better Than One

No doubt you've heard the virtues of teamwork to complete a task or an important project. But thinking? That's something you do by yourself and inside your own head, right? Maybe not.

Research shows that problem-solving in a group or as part of a pair is more effective than flying solo. It may be all very well to come up with ideas by yourself, but truly successful people depend on an intellectual equal to help vet their ideas before any important decisions are made.

In their seminal paper, "Why Do Humans Reason? Arguments for an Argumentative Theory," French social scientists Dan Sperber and Hugo Mercier posited that thinking and reasoning have an important component that disproportionately improves outcomes. This key component is arguing. It's obviously difficult to uncover unbiased inputs when you argue with yourself. This is where a mental sparring partner comes in. Think of it as adding a yin to your yang so you can arrive at your "eureka!" moment.

Nature backs this theory of collective problem-solving. A study from the School of Biological Sciences at the University of Sydney revealed that shoals of fish solve problems faster and more accurately than individual fish: "Shoals containing individuals trained in each of the stages pooled their expertise, allowing more fish to access the food, and to do so more rapidly, compared with other shoal compositions."

Even Warren Buffett relies on the sharp insights of Berkshire Hathaway vice chairman Charlie Munger. It's probably a good idea to include a business partner or even a close team into your ideation process and problem-solving model.

Culture Impacts Your Ability to Solve Problems

Involving one or more teammates in a problem-solving process may not be enough. You need individuals with minds of their own. These unique points of view allow for a variety of ideas and approaches. Second—and more important—each independent thinker needs to feel free to contribute their thoughts without fear of ridicule or retribution.

A cognitively diverse team brings together people with completely different approaches to solving the same problem. You're looking for a range of people: analytical types, creatives, and organized discipline-maintainers. Because each offers something distinct, the team comes up with a rich variety of ideas to consider.

The team should have the opportunity to function in a psychologically safe space. Here's how it looks in real life: Members are encouraged to contribute without hesitation, mistakes are looked on as opportunities to get better, and the team moves faster and is open to experimentation. The result? An environment emerges that's ripe for path-breaking solutions and quicker, more efficient processes.

Global Diversity for the Win

What do SpaceX, Uber, and Stripe have in common? Aside from being billion-dollar startups, each of these American companies has founders who were born outside the United States. In fact, a National Foundation for American Policy brief pointed out that 51 percent of all billion-dollar startups in the U.S. in 2016 were founded or co-founded by immigrants.

Research led by William Maddux, a professor of organizational behavior at INSEAD, explains this phenomenon. A series of experiments found that foreign-born participants or those who'd lived abroad for substantial lengths of time solved problems more quickly and creatively.

The researchers explained that individuals are forced to leverage their creativity and problem-solving skills to adapt to a foreign culture and customs. This constant adjustment and thinking on one's feet make such individuals uniquely well equipped to devise creative solutions to problems. Undoubtedly, these evolved problem-solving skills contribute to success in business.

So what do you do? Move to a different country and start a new business there? Probably not.

You could start by hiring a diverse work force that includes people across different nationalities. These varied voices and eclectic mindsets have the potential to revamp your problem-solving process and offer a much-needed fresh perspective.

In times of need, resourceful business owners can find plenty of problem-solving templates. But the beaten path often is the quickest route to failure. Instead, opt for a more original and creative journey. The road may be more winding and cumbersome, but science proves that going the extra mile helps you solve problems more efficiently. Stretching that extra neuron just might make you smarter along the way!

CHAPTER SIX

How to Overcome Discouragement

J. Martin Kohe

J. Martin Kohe is best known as the author of *Your Greatest Power*, which is published by the Napoleon Hill Foundation. This small book has sold over a million copies, and even though it was first published in 1953, it continues to sell well today.

Your Greatest Power has a wonderful message about our power to choose. Many people cannot be successful in the best of times because they do not recognize their power to choose their own life.

J. Martin Kohe was a psychologist and gave many lectures about becoming a mental millionaire, which were later published into a book. Kohe also recorded an audio called "How to Overcome Discouragement," which is featured below.

By reading this selection from Kohe, it is not hard to realize that he truly understood the mind was the solution to leading a better life.

❧ ❧ ❧

AVOID PERFECTION SYNDROME

Criticism does not come into your life to make you weaker but to make you stronger. Another very important principle in the subject of criticism is something that very, very few people realize. As you probably remember from your school days, you studied about the Gulf Stream. The Gulf Stream is a hot body of water that runs along the coast of Florida and up and around England. If it were not for this hot body of water, people would not be able to live in England, and Florida would not be so inviting. The Gulf Stream, without anyone paying attention to it, runs its course. Likewise, there is a Gulf Stream running through your life and my life seeking perfection.

It seems that everyone is seeking perfection. Consequently, the wife criticizes the husband because she wants him to be perfect. The husband criticizes the wife because he wants her to be perfect. The parent criticizes the child because he wants the child to be perfect. The child criticizes the parents because he wants the parents to be perfect. The teacher criticizes the student because he wants the student to be perfect. The student criticizes the teacher because he wants the teacher to be perfect. A boss criticizes the worker because he wants the worker to be perfect, and the worker criticizes the boss because he wants the boss to be perfect. The minister criticizes the congregation because he wants them to be perfect. And the congregation criticizes the minister because they want him to be perfect. Everybody seems to be criticizing everybody else. You wonder why life sometimes is so difficult. Don't ask your boss, your wife, or your child to be perfect. If they are reasonably perfect, you are a very fortunate person. Don't even ask yourself to be perfect. If you are reasonably perfect, you should be quite happy with yourself. This constant demanding of perfection on ourselves and others is one of the greatest discouraging factors in life.

It's quite all right to ask for a perfect typewriter or automobile or something of a mechanical nature, but when you ask it of a human being, you are making an unreasonable demand. Save yourself much trouble and great discouragement in the years to come. Simply ask yourself this question: Am I criticizing simply because I want perfection? If so, be more reasonable. When someone criticizes you, ask the question: Are they doing it because they want me to be perfect? Then discount it. It's quite all right to seek perfection, but in dealing with yourself and others, make sure that you are reasonable.

LIGHTEN UP

One of the greatest of all destructive forces in the discussion of discouragement is that of being too serious. Life is a serious business, but life can also be made enjoyable and very much worthwhile; but when one takes life too seriously, then there is no room for pleasure or enjoyment for real living. We are going through life only once, although some authorities seem to feel we may go through it again. I, for one, feel that if we do go through it again, we won't know about it. Let us make this one time that we are going through life really worthwhile. In order to do that, we must learn how to laugh. We must learn to see the funny side of life. We must train ourselves more than anything else to throw off the seriousness that seems constantly to disturb our living. Unless we accomplish this task, we will look older and feel much older than our actual years.

It was Lincoln who said, "A man is just about as happy as he makes up his mind to be." Contrary to general belief, we do not find happiness. We *earn* it. We earn it by constantly watching our thinking. One man who has achieved much throughout his life is Winston Churchill. When he was asked the question, "How do you keep yourself calm with all that you have to do?" He replied, "I think of only one thing at a time." That is the monumental key to the right mental attitude. If you realize that you can think of only one thing at a time, then by thinking of something pleasant, you keep yourself pleasant. By thinking of something cheerful, you keep yourself cheerful. By thinking of something unhappy, you make yourself unhappy, and if you think of something discouraging, of course, you will find yourself discouraged.

Does this sound too simple? Of course it does, but it works and you will find so many of these suggestions and ideas that we are presenting to you will work if you work them. Wherever possible, never take yourself or anyone else too seriously. This is one of the great destroyers of mankind and of our thinking. Be serious, but not too serious. Learn to laugh. You'll find that it will come easier with practice.

AGREE TO DISAGREE

It seems no matter what you do or how you do it, you cannot satisfy everybody. There is one way, however, that this great problem of human relations can be satisfactorily taken care of. We have so many differences of opinion and yet we have a semblance of order that is something to be proud of.

Please stop thinking it is wrong to disagree with others. If Edison had not disagreed with the rest of the world when he did, we wouldn't have had electric lights when we had them. There is nothing wrong with disagreement. We must always bear in mind what a wise old sage said many years ago: "If we must disagree, let us disagree without being disagreeable." Oh, if we could only learn this one great principle of life. To disagree without being disagreeable, we could avoid most of the very unhappy experiences we have in dealing with people. This is especially true with people who have put on years. Too many people grow old and with the growing old grow more disagreeable. If we could only learn to grow in sweetness, in friendliness, in helpfulness, the passing years would not be so difficult. When we think of sweetness, we always associate it with childhood because we see so little of it in people of advanced years. If people would only learn to age instead of growing old, they could retain the sweetness of life. They would not become so discouraged as they add years to their lives. A person should make up his mind to enjoy the 50s, the 60s, the 70s, and the 80s. He can if he will train himself. He can train himself to enjoy the later years in life as much as he did when he was much younger. A person in his 50s and 60s now has lived long enough to be able to think so much better than a child of 12 or 14.

It's important that we watch ourselves carefully so that we disagree without being disagreeable. When we can do that, we will never be alone. People will want us around. Children will have much greater respect for us. More than anything else, we will have greater respect for ourselves.

DON'T GIVE UP SO QUICKLY

Another factor leading to discouragement is giving up too soon. Too many people allow themselves to become discouraged, and then give up just before it is time to see success come their way. It was Elbert Hubbard who said, "Many times there's just a line between success and failure." Too many people go right up to that line and then drop away. Had they kept right on going, they would have reached the other side, the success side. Remember the story of the man who ended his life by taking gas because some money that was coming to him did not come when it was supposed to? Thinking that the money was not forthcoming, he ended his life. The very next day, the check came in.

But the classic story of quitting too soon is the story that Napoleon Hill tells in his famous book, *Think and Grow Rich*. Darby went out west and discovered a gold mine. He worked the mine with pick and shovel for several months then came to the conclusion that this was not the right way to go about it. So he covered up the mine after staking his claim, went back to his home in the east and there he talked to his friends and relatives and neighbors. He told them about the gold mine, explaining that if he had mining machinery, he and they would all make plenty of money. They agreed. They put up the money for the machinery. The machinery was bought and sent to the spot of the mine. The machinery was started, and just as Darby expected, there was plenty of gold. He started to pay off the debts on the land and on the machinery. He was just about ready to start to save some money for himself when the mine ran dry.

"Well," Darby thought, "there is no sense in staying here anymore." So he called in a junk man, sold the machinery for junk, and threw the deed of the mine in with it. But it so happened that this junk man was no fool, and he called in a mining engineer. The engineer was to examine the mine and make out his report to the junk man. The junk man told the engineer that if the mine was worthless, he would break up the machinery and sell it for junk. But he wanted to be sure.

The engineer went down into the mine, made a thorough search of the mine, and made out his report to the junk man. What do you suppose he found? The report said that all the junk man had to do was find the secondary vein of gold, and he would find his gold mine if he would dig three feet deeper. The junk man started the machinery, and sure enough, three feet deeper they found the secondary vein of gold and the junk man became the millionaire.

In the meantime, Darby had returned to his home in the east, and when he heard what happened to his gold mine, he almost lost his own mind. After a year, however, Darby recovered from this awful shock and went into another business. Every time he felt like quitting, he said to himself, "Wait a minute, Darby. Wait a minute. You may be only 3 feet away from the very thing you want." With this awful, terrible experience behind him, Darby became a very wealthy man in another field of work. Remember next time you want to quit anything, be very sure that you are not three 3 away from the very thing you want.

ALWAYS HAVE AN EXIT STRATEGY

Another factor causing discouragement is that of feeling that there is nothing that can be done about a given situation. Some years ago in the city of Chicago, a young newspaper reporter was called in by his boss and told that if he did not go out and bring in some stories that he would be fired from his job. The young man left the paper that night fearful of losing his job and proceeded to get himself drunk. He got so drunk that he wound up lying in the curb, dead drunk. As he lay there, he noticed a sewer manhole cover being raised and coming out of the sewer were three people. One was dressed like a prince. One was dressed like a king, and one was dressed like a princess.

When he saw all this, he thought surely he was having hallucinations. He picked himself up and finally wiggled his way home.

The next morning, he went downstairs and bought a morning paper. In screaming headlines he read of the big Chicago fire. These three people were not hallucinations. They were real people. What happened was that a fire broke out in a theatre. These three people were downstairs in the basement. When they heard there was a fire in the theater proper, they opened the door and noticed that it led into the sewer. They continued in the sewer until they saw a manhole, then came up to the street through the manhole.

> ● **ENTREPRENEUR TIP**
>
> Can't get out of your discouragement rut? Focus on what is immediate instead of trying to solve a big problem all at once. When facing a complicated problem, make a quick list of two to three small things you can do to help overcome it. Often, big problems are just a series of small problems that are lumped together. Eat the elephant one bite at a time so you can make progress and overcome those feelings of discouragement.

I am sure that you see the point of this story. Just as those three people found a way out of that theater fire, so you will find there is always a way out of your troubles. If you keep yourself calm, you will find the right way out. If you let yourself get upset and excited, you will find the wrong way out. Yes, as awful and as destructive as discouragement can be, there is always a way out, a better way out. A better way of life and a better mental attitude to make life worth the living.

PERSEVERANCE IS KEY

Now I would like to close with a classic story that tells so much to all of us. The story is told about two frogs. They were playing around a vat of cream. Before they realized what had happened, they both fell into the vat. One of the frogs, after swimming for a while said, "This will never do. I'll never get out of this mess," so he sank to the bottom and that was his end. The second frog said, "No, I'll keep swimming until I don't have an ounce of strength left." So he kept on swimming and swimming and swimming and finally that vat of cream turned into a vat of butter. Then the second frog found himself sitting high and dry on top of the vat of butter. Yes, my friends. If we choose to keep on going, keep on swimming, keep on digging 3 feet deeper, we will win the struggle with discouragement. Once we do, life can be a grand and glorious venture.

⚜ ENTREPRENEUR ACTION ITEM
15 Ways to Drown Out Discouragement

To reach your goals, you have to take risks, develop constructive routines, and make time to listen, learn, and reflect. The prospect of making any of the above adjustments to your life is empowering—that is, until your mind starts to wander toward negative thoughts.

Any time you've thought about making a change or pursuing a passion, you've probably dwelled more on your present state than your potential. Or once you got started, minor setbacks or flubs have felt like deal-breaking failures. You've beaten yourself up, berated yourself, or felt overwhelmed or alone.

Constant reminders of other people's triumphs only make you feel more anxious and criticize yourself further. Whether you're scrolling through your Instagram feed or reading about a competitor, your knee-jerk reaction to someone else's success might be a combination of envy and self-loathing. A cascade of negative thoughts can produce negative outcomes: Inaction. Retreat. Bad habits. By thinking negatively about what you will accomplish, you formulate a self-fulfilling prophecy.

You're not inadequate or doomed to fail. So next time you're thinking some variation of those negative thoughts, try these 15 strategies to propel yourself out of your funk and proceed with the mission you've set out to achieve.

1. *What you tell yourself:* "I don't know when or how I'm going to do this."
   What you should think or do instead: Set a schedule.
Set aside time each day or week to work toward your goal. Then stick to your plan. Create a calendar slot for it, and treat it as nonoptional, like a job. Eventually, you'll form a new, positive habit.

2. *What you tell yourself:* "I'm not in the right environment."
   What you should think or do instead: Carve out a corner.
That doubting, destructive voice in your head will find any excuse to impede your progress toward your goal. It's easy to blame your environment, but there are ways to make your circumstances work for you—or create new ones.

Once you establish a positive, dedicated place, it will be easier to tune out other aspects of your life while you're working toward your goal. When you're sitting in your corner, surrounded by inspirational objects, or at your new table in your community space, you'll have physically and mentally removed yourself from the place where you also pay bills, eat dinner, or help your kids with homework.

3. *What you tell yourself:* "I'm not in the mood."
   What you should think or do instead: "Procrastinate with purpose."
Make "put it off" time work for you. Find other ways to be productive that not only knock items off your to-do list, but also recharge your personal and professional batteries. Fill your time with productive tasks that will indirectly lead you toward your goal.

4. *What you tell yourself:* "I don't know what to do next. I feel stuck."
   What you should think or do instead: Relax and take your time.
Working toward a goal often involves decision making, tackling difficult tasks, and making tough sacrifices. Often, when faced with these dilemmas, people feel pressure to resolve them quickly, but they aren't always sure about the best course of action.

First, try to relax and take it step by step. Write down your thoughts—what you like about a potential decision vs. what you dread about it. Forgive yourself for not taking the next step yet. Chances are, you'll have a more positive end result if you give yourself time.

5. *What you tell yourself:* "I will never achieve my goal."
   What you should think or do instead: Tell yourself the opposite.
So you've had a setback in your quest to achieve your goal. You know you shouldn't insult yourself, but you can't stop. Your thoughts become more and more negative, maybe until you convince yourself of something terribly untrue, such as "you're worthless," or "you'll never achieve your goal."

Your failure to execute on your goals up to this point is not a reflection of your character. The fact that you've formed a goal in the first place indicates that you have an idea of how to better yourself or add something positive to the world. Now you have to do it, and the biggest obstacle in your way might be yourself and that nagging voice telling you there's something wrong with you or that you can't.

6. *What you tell yourself:* "I'm a total mess."
   What you should think or do instead: Organize the little details of your life to prime yourself for your big goal.

It's easy to get bogged down by the small things, such as how you look, how clogged your inbox is, or how many errands you've been putting off. Disorganization in minor aspects of your personal life could deter you from thinking you're ready to take on something big.

Prepare as much as you can. That way, you can focus on bigger hurdles.

7. *What you tell yourself:* "My goal is stupid."
   What you should think or do instead: Exude confidence bordering on arrogance.

If you're preoccupied with the idea that no one else will be interested in what you're trying to do, you may start trying to convince yourself that you should quit pursuing your goal based on what you're worried others will think.

Try to avoid beating yourself up. Instead, try to learn from your mistakes and understand that confidence is everything. Take up space, and practice good posture if that helps you realize your own confidence. Both can reinforce positive self-perception. Despite the fact that science has not proved power posing effective, some people find that it has a positive effect on their confidence.

8. *What you tell yourself:* "That other person already achieved my goal and made it look so easy. I'll never be as good as them."
   What you should think or do instead: Approach the person and ask for advice.

It can be toxic to think about other people's success. You may put them on a pedestal and think they're superhuman or free of doubt. Ultimately, you may become wildly jealous of them to the point that you devalue yourself and your potential.

You shouldn't feel shy about reaching out to someone you feel inferior to. The other person probably has similar thoughts, and you have plenty to teach them, too.

9. *What you tell yourself:* "Even if I achieve my goal, I'm never going to impress the people I want to impress."

   What you should think or do instead: I'm here to connect with others.

Reaching a goal, especially a professional one, is often about more than your ability to excel in your line of work. It also involves a social element, such as networking. This leaves many people convinced that they are going to make a negative impression. Someone will find them too shy, too bossy, too *something* and not enough *something else*, and that deficiency will cloud all their achievements, so they think.

Try not to focus on the worst version of yourself or on the self you wish you could be. Try instead to think about how you act around those who value you the most and mirror that behavior elsewhere. Approach meetings and social events with an interest in others, rather than a preoccupation with yourself and your own shortcomings.

10. *What you tell yourself:* "It doesn't seem like I'm making any progress toward my goal."

    What you should think or do instead: Find someone to hold you accountable.

When you take on a new challenge, it can be discouraging when your life doesn't magically change overnight. You're working so hard, yet you don't feel like you're getting anywhere. You begin to wonder if all your effort is worth it.

To ensure you don't give up on your goal, establish a support system—one person or a group who will hold you accountable. It could be a family member; Facebook friends, or a life coach. You'll feel less alone in your journey, you'll have someone to report to who will make sure you follow through, and best of all, you'll have someone who will notice and remind you of how far you've come.

11. *What you tell yourself:* "That didn't work."

    What you should think or do instead: Keep your goal, but find a new means of achieving it.

It's one thing to be oblivious of the subtle progress you're making, it's another to know that what you're doing is ineffective. But rather than give up in those times, try a different approach.

Say you're trying to learn a new skill. For example, you might be trying to learn a new language solely by listening to audio guides during your commute, but you're not a strong auditory learner. So, you may need to rethink your approach. Perhaps, you learn better with an app or gamification.

12. *What you tell yourself:* "This goal isn't enough. I should be doing more."
   What you should think or do instead: Focus.
Don't overload yourself with to-dos. If you're making a little progress, don't devalue what you've already accomplished by trying to take on a new task or goal. It's likely that you still have work to do on the first one.

Instead, recognize that you should just focus on one thing at a time.

13. *What you tell yourself:* "I'm so overwhelmed."
   What you should think or do instead: Journal.
Goal-setting requires focus. You have to stay organized about what you need to do to achieve your goal, but you can't shut the world out, nor can you always resist the temptation to get ahead of yourself. When there are a lot of thoughts swirling around in your head (including negative ones), it can help to write some of them down.

Write just one or two things most days, whether it's something you want to work toward or something that's been on your mind. There's no structure or plan for what you can write down—just record your thoughts.

Writing things down also gives you the chance to reflect. You can go back later bimonthly and read your notes to resurface thoughts, do follow ups, and remember things that were done well.

14. *What you tell yourself:* "Working toward this goal is taking over my life."
   What you should think or do instead: Take care of yourself.
A lot of people who are working hard toward a goal, be it a college degree or a company launch, let their wellness go by the wayside. They romanticize all-nighters and ramen noodles and think that the more they're sacrificing for their goal, the more likely they are to reach it.

While some people succeed despite neglecting their own health, it is not sustainable for most.

If you're not paying attention to your nutrition, it is going to affect your ability to think clearly. Similarly, stagnation in the body correlates with stagnation in the mind—and creativity.

Don't be afraid to invest some time to burn some energy and take care of yourself by eating right and sleeping.

15. *What you tell yourself:* "I'm scared to face the changes that achieving my goal will bring."

What you should think or do instead: It's not a matter of life or death. Think of the most intimidating thing you've had to face or the most dangerous situation you've had to get out of. Now recognize that you made it. You're here, right now, reading this.

Now think of your goal, and think of which aspect of reaching it is so scary to you. Compare that with what you've already overcome in your life. Finally, know that it's natural to fear new things. Humans are creatures of habit. But they also tend to beat themselves up. You'll continue to do that if you don't take the plunge toward what you're trying to achieve.

CHAPTER SEVEN

Facing Life Successfully

Earl Nightingale

What does it take to face the facts of your life? Overcoming problems and adversity is an essential part of any success plan, and no one knows that better than motivational author Earl Nightingale. Born at the dawn of the Great Depression, Nightingale was raised by a single mother and later went on to a successful radio career. Later, after being inspired by Napoleon Hill's *Think and Grow Rich*, Nightingale began his career as a motivational speaker and writer. He later went on to start the Nightingale-Conant Corp. with Lloyd

Conant, which remains one of the biggest sellers of motivational content. He died in 1989.

Here, in this essay, Nightingale discusses how you can rise to face life's challenges.

❦ ❦ ❦

THE ANSWER IS IN THE PROBLEM

The first point I want to make is that all of us have problems, and that our problems will only end when we confront them. We have national problems, corporate problems, family problems, personal problems. But there are two Chinese symbols that together form the ideograph for opportunity. One stands for trouble, the other for crisis. Trouble and crisis, when put together, represent opportunity. As the answer always lies in the question, so the opportunities of life lie directly in our problems. It's one of the most difficult things in the world to learn, but it is absolutely true. And in the problem itself always lies the answer to that problem.

RISK EQUALS REWARD

A great American educator, Arthur E. Morgan, noted that the process of constantly pressing upon one's limits is what makes life become larger. That habit can become one of the chief sources of enjoyment and interest in our lives. Those who find themselves bored and unhappy as the years progress and finally come to the end of their lives querulous and bitter, are those who have never discovered the joys of pressing themselves, of searching for sources of strength, talent, and interest far beyond the safe and placid boundaries of their day-to-day experiences.

I gave some flowers the other day to my assistant, and she commented that they were very beautiful. "But," she said, "you know, they don't smell good." And so I explained to her that flowers which are raised in a hothouse environment, where everything is done for them, simply don't have to attract insects anymore to pollinate themselves, so they lose their scent. It's the same with fruit that's raised under these same kind of circumstances: They don't taste as good as the apple we pick from a tree. They don't have to work hard to attract animals and birds to spread their seed.

When my son and I were visiting Australia's Great Barrier Reef this past March, we were amazed to discover, as we were told there, that the coral polyps in the inside of the reef, where they're protected, where the water is calm, tend to die and fall apart, while the coral polyps on the outside of the reef, where the breakers are pounding on them every day and every night, thrive and reproduce marvelously. Now what I'm getting at is that we, too, are creatures. We are related to the coral polyps. And the human creature thrives at his very best in a climate of risk. One of the paradoxes of modern life is that the thing the human being seeks most assiduously, a state of complete security, so called, is the very state that's the worst for him. He is at his best and is happiest when he's working, stretching, reaching, trying to achieve new and more difficult goals. It's just the way it is.

Of the millions of creatures that have appeared on this planet, more than 90 percent have become extinct. They could not handle change. They could not cope with risk. Marriages tend to survive the risks and hardships of working toward meaningful goals. It's when the goal has been reached that they fall apart. I wonder how many couples have said, wistfully, "You know, we were happier when we were living in that walk-up flat and working our tails off."

DON'T SIT ON YOUR GOALS

There's a great educator by the name of Sidney Hook, who taught for many years at Columbia University, who said a very wise thing. He said that while anticipation is a marvelous thing and motivates us, the real disasters in life occur when we get what we want. Now, I want to modify that a little bit. There's nothing wrong with reaching our goals, unless we sit on them. Unless we stop there. And when we stop, we begin the process of dissolution, of falling apart. How do we know the true range of our growing capacities, and that the capacity of a 50-year-old man is greater than the capacity of a 45-year-old man, and so on? How do we know the true range of our growing capacities unless we keep pressing toward those goals that tend to fulfill us as persons, whatever they are? Whatever you happen to desire.

I saw a very funny cartoon in the *The Wall Street Journal* not long ago. It showed two men standing on a busy corner in New York. One was dressed in a business suit, the other was wearing a toga, sandals, horn-rim glasses, and carrying a briefcase. And the one in the toga is saying to the other man, "I've found enlightenment, and I still pull down my 85 thousand a year." Now, it seems that that will work for us. We can do both. We can reach the goals that we want and we can still find the fulfillment, the peace, and these other things that we would also like to have.

Now, it seems that as a species, collectively, we tend to want things as human beings that aren't good for us when a marvelous balance of maturity and education is missing. We do that as a species simply because the great majority of human beings lack the education and insight into what makes the human being happy and successful. And the majority constitutes a tremendous influence on us all.

AVOID GROUPTHINK

Freud and others discovered that there is a basic human dread of leaving the security of the family and venturing forth alone into the mysteries and dangers of the world. By belonging to a group (the larger the better), we're able to maintain the feeling of security and protection we knew as small children. These feelings are embedded in one's earliest experiences of comfortable merger with the family. People want to be led. They want others to make the important decisions for them, and they're willing to pay for the leadership they get, no matter how expensive or wrongheaded it may be.

> ### ◈ ENTREPRENEUR TIP
>
> Want to be a part of a group without giving in to groupthink? Create a coalition of people in your industry and find a time each month to meet up and discuss common concerns and issues that affect your business. By reaching out to colleagues outside of your own business, you can talk about those issues without the concern of interoffice politics affecting the conversations.

How many times have you sat in a restaurant, and everyone's holding a menu, and one of them says, "What are you having?" He just simply can't make up his mind. He wants you to order for him. I've seen people at stop lights, that even after it turns green, they won't go until another car goes and indicates that it's OK to go ahead and pull out. It's why most businesses look alike, as well as the people who run them and think alike, too. They wait for ideas to come from the home office or pick them up at the annual convention.

OK, there's a powerful human tendency to think that others are quite qualified to do our thinking for us. Perhaps we never think of it quite that way, but that's what it amounts to. But there are at least two very excellent reasons for questioning that idea and examining from time to time the present course of our lives and thinking. We can think as well as anyone else.

The first is that we tend to settle for too small a portion of the richness, the real richness of life, and in fact usually don't even know the true direction to follow. As Americans, we often as not believe the answers are to be found in the collection of things. But as we pile things on top of things and new things on top of other things, we often find that we're not finding the happiness we sought. As one writer put it, 'We have built a technological tower to the moon, but as we look down from the top of our leaning tower, we find that we're no nearer heaven and that perhaps we'd better return to earth again."

In Ernest Becker's excellent Pulitzer Prize winning book, *The Denial of Death*, which I strongly recommend, he points out that in our immaturity we pile things on top of things because they give us symbolic reinforcement of our value as persons. They tell us how wonderful we are and in our immaturity we need that. When we hear of a pipeline explosion at a pumping station on the Alaska Pipeline, or an airplane disaster, we all seem to be oddly relieved when we hear someone say, "It was a human error." To know that our beloved machines were not to blame. The crowning proof of where modern science rates the human creature vis-a-vis other things was beautifully clarified, I think, by the development of the neutron bomb: It just kills people; it doesn't damage the real estate.

The second important thing to remember is that until we get the human being back in first place, back on the very top of the pile of values, we're not going to have our heads on straight. Everything we do, all our work, all of our striving and education and scientific investigation, every business and government agency exists in order to help men, woman and children lead better, more interesting, healthier, and effective and satisfying lives. When we get that straight, everything else has a way of falling into place.

I remember hearing about a man who was watching television one Sunday afternoon, watching a football game. And his little boy, about 5 years old, kept bothering him, and so he reached down to the Sunday paper and there was a full-page ad for TWA there, with a big picture of the globe. And he tore it up in little pieces and gave the boy the torn-up picture and some Scotch tape and he said, "See if you can put the world together for Daddy." In just a couple of minutes, the boy came back with the whole thing put together, and he was astounded. He said, "How in the world did you do that?" And the boy said, "Well, there was a picture of a man on the other side, and when I got him together, the world was OK."

We have a tendency to think that whatever people are doing in large numbers must be right because so many of them are doing it. As with so many popular beliefs, it turns out that just the opposite is true. One of the great American financiers and advisors to presidents, Bernard Baruch, was once asked by a reporter the for the secret of his success. And he smiled, the wise old man, and he said, "I buy my straw hats in the fall."

Here's a rule of thumb to keep in mind: Whatever the great majority of people is doing under any given circumstance, if you'll do exactly the opposite, you will probably never make another mistake as long as you live. I have never yet found an exception to that rule. It applies to getting an education, decorating your home, raising your children, handling your work, driving your car. As E.F. Schumacher has pointed out, millions slave in mindless and mind-rotting work without question, simply because others around them are doing the same thing. So collectively, we tend to want things that aren't good for us when the balance is missing.

AVOID THE EFFECTS OF AFFLUENCE

It's been only during the past few seconds of our species' existence on this planet that we've experienced general affluence, and only in this country. It's something new, even to the United States and Canada. For most of the rest of the world, it's still something to dream about and work toward, yet it's a sociological fact of life today in America that the American people are not happier now than they were during the Great Depression of the '30s. Now, that's obviously not because they were poor; they were happier than one might expect because they knew where they were going, what they were working toward. They had meaningful goals. They were striving, they were living in the state of risk.

Affluence, in many ways, has sickened us as a society, as it will sicken any society, as it sickened the ancient Roman society and made it into a soft, overripe plum ready for picking by the hungry hordes. Affluence without corresponding wisdom and maturity makes the human creature ridiculous. There is nothing more ludicrous, more pitiful, than the human being who thinks he already knows enough. Affluence causes us, if we're ill-equipped to handle it, to lose sight of what's important and what isn't. We tend to forget what brought affluence in the first place, which was meaningful, quality production that made this nation strong and the miracle that it became. It was productivity, hard work, and meaningful goals. Production, ladies and gentlemen, is the key to the solution to our problems as a nation, as a community, as a family, and as individuals. Meaningful, intelligent production, quality production, and if possible, with flair.

Now, the United States has softened in certain areas, as we've found by the productivity and inventiveness of Japan and West Germany and France, and some other countries which are striving very hard to get what we've got. We still lead in many, in most important areas, and we're waking up in many others. General Motors will spend over a billion dollars in R&D (research and development) this year, as will IBM. Being successful should never be confused with remaining successful; those are two distinctly different animals. And may I respectfully inquire how much you, as a person, are spending on R&D this year? How much of your take-home pay are you pumping back into quality products calculated to make you a more intelligent, creative, productive human creature?

MAKE UP YOUR MIND

You know, once we decide on what we really want, we're certainly amazed at how little it really is. And then we discover that we can have what we want. We can have everything we want, if we'll simply make up our minds as to what it is. People don't have trouble achieving their goals; their difficulties stem from not setting them, from drifting, from being subject to every vague wind, every breeze and tide. We're like ships, quite often, without rudders, subject to every wind and tide. Let me suggest that you turn your car into a learning center, that you listen while you're driving. Build your office and home library of books. Spend an hour a day in the lonely hours reading, thinking, listening, setting goals, making notes, coming up with new and better, more effective, more creative ways of doing a better job of serving those you have chosen of your own free will to serve. If you'll do that, you need have no worries about the future.

> ⚙ ENTREPRENEUR TIP
> We are living in the golden age of content. There is so much information out there (on any topic) that it's like drinking from a firehose. To focus your learning patterns, curate your content around topics that interest you right now. One great way to do that is to choose a topic each month, then build yourself a reading and podcast list that reflects that theme.

I hope I didn't give the impression that I'm anti-technology; I'm not. There are some towering and exciting problems that need solving in the world right now, and I'd like very much to see the United States solve more of them, and I think we can expect that. I believe that very soon now, we will find, we will develop an alternative fuel that will liberate the whole world from the domination of an anachronistic fossil fuel, and then the oil barons can try selling sand. As far as we know, there's very little market for sand today. But we must keep technology in its place. It's exciting, it's wonderful, it's scary at times. It's awful, too, as we find new and more efficient ways to destroy ourselves. But there's nothing on Earth, ladies and gentlemen, more important than a human creature. A little girl or boy or an old man or woman, of any color whatever, in any country on this planet.

DEFINE HAPPINESS

Let me give you the definition of happiness. It's the best one I've ever found. It was given to us by a man believed by some to be the smartest man who ever lived, John Stuart Mill. It goes like this: "Those only are happy who have their minds fixed on some object other than their own happiness. On the happiness of others, on the improvement of mankind, even on some art or pursuit, followed not as a means but as itself an ideal end." That's the secret. Aiming at something else, he concluded, people find happiness by the way. It's only when we're doing something as an end in itself that happiness, like a butterfly, comes and settles on our sleeve.

Now in closing, a couple of reminders. Quality production is the answer. Production, good, quality production as a person. The great Abraham Maslow, president of the American Psychological Association, used to say that, "You judge a human being the same way you judge an apple tree: by its production."

And Dean Briggs put it this way. He said, "Do your work. Not just your work and no more, but a little more than is expected. That little more is worth all the rest. And if you doubt, as you must, and if you suffer, as you must, do your work. Put your heart into it and the sky will clear. And then, out of your very doubt and suffering, will be born the supreme joy of life." Believe it or not, that's where it is.

SET GOALS AND BE A LIFELONG LEARNER

Number two, set goals. Goals that are worthy of you.

Three, keep that education going, every day, a little bit. Learn to be a little smarter, a little gentler, a little kinder, a little more effective every day as a human creature. You'll never be bored, and you'll never get old. Our education should end when we do, and not one day before.

This kind of an education I'm talking about will help us learn to love what doesn't cost much, and to love reading and conversation and music, and to do our work as well as we can learn to do it. To become professionals in a world of amateurs. To love people, even though they're quite different from us. To love life for its own sake and to love the sunrise and the sunset and the beating of rain on the roof and windows, or the gentle fall of snow on a winter day. This kind of an education helps us learn to love the companionship of dogs and the laughter and gaiety of children. But most of all, this kind of a daily education in those lonely hours will teach us to be free. Free from blind and mindless conformity, from tribalism and superstition, from the domination of things and the opinions of others.

Education is the process by which we narrow the gap between where we are and what we are, and what we want to be and become. A great American educator, Dr. Gilbert Hiatt of Columbia University, said, "Wholeness of mind and spirit is not a quality conferred on us by nature or by God. It is like health, virtue, and knowledge: We have the capacity to attain it, but to achieve it depends on our own efforts."

In your dealing with people of all ages (little, tiny children, old people, everybody in between), remember they want three things more than anything else in the world, and so do you and I. And they want them in this order of importance. Number one: They want recognition, the opposite of anonymity, more than anything in the world. Recognize them, listen to them, look at them and they'll bloom like flowers in a garden. Two: They want stimulation and change, the opposite of boredom. Keep things changing. Don't let things settle down to the dull, dreary ruts of boredom. And three: They want security. But it's in third place, and there are several kinds of security. They want to be secure in our love, secure in our word, secure in our integrity, the product we sell, the people we are. Let's give them what they want, and they'll respond marvelously.

And let me close with this little poem written by one of my favorite poets, the Nobel Prize-winning poet from Calcutta, Rabindranath Thakur: *"I slept and dreamt that life was joy. I woke and saw that life was duty. I acted and behold, duty was joy."*

Believe it or not, ladies and gentlemen, that's it.

⚜ ENTREPRENEUR ACTION ITEM
How to Live with Purpose and Stay Focused on Long-Term Goals

Nightingale reminds us to set goals that are worthy of us. In other words, set goals that enrich both your business and your life for the long term. Let's think about it this way. Your habits are broken down into two categories: instant pleasure and delayed. Everyone has some instant habits, things like social media or TV or squeezing your dog's squishy face, and everyone has some delayed habits that connect to your bigger-picture visions of health, happiness, and wealth. That's normal. All balanced humans have both.

But if you're hungry for more purpose, happiness, wealth, and meaning, you've got to be long-term dominant. There's no other way around it. And that means learning how to plan.

Without an action-packed daily plan that connects you to your future, you'll automatically fill your time with mostly instant pleasure, like social media, watching videos, or reading inspiring articles. Instant pleasure is great, don't get me wrong. But like sweets, it's best after you've eaten your main meal and only in small doses.

The thing is, most people don't know what their main meal is. So they go through their day hungry for purpose and needing direction, then they settle for occupations of their time that don't lead to tangible gains. Instead of doing that, think about how you can form a better, stronger way to achieve your goals, one day at a time. Here are some steps you can take to make those long-term goals a reality.

Get Crystal Clarity on Your Yearly Goals

What career do you want to be in? Where do you want to be in your health and fitness journey? What fun and self-love goals would make this the best year of your life? What do you want to learn? What are your financial goals? And how do you plan on giving back? These are the six major areas that your goals will fall into. So have a seat and write out each category:

- Career
- Health/fitness
- Fun/self-love
- Learning
- Financial
- Giving

Then meditate on exactly what you want in each of those categories. Write those goals down. That's your yearly planner—you'll reflect on this every time you do a monthly planning strategy.

Set a Recurring Date for Monthly Strategy Sessions

You'd be surprised at how many people lack clarity on their long-term vision. But of those who do know what they want, hardly any of them will take the time to break down their "elephants" into smaller, more digestible chunks. So you have a bunch of people with awesome dreams like "I'm going to write for *The New York Times!*" and their action steps look like this:

"Write for *The New York Times!*"

That lofty goal must be broken down into sections that can be accomplished month by month; otherwise it just won't happen. The same is true for whatever goals you have in mind. So give yourself 30 minutes to an hour each month for a monthly planning session. During this recurring appointment with yourself (which is best done on Sundays), you'll reflect on your long-term goals and your notes, and you'll brainstorm realistic milestones that can be achieved in 30 days.

For the fictitious *New York Times* writing goal, that might involve writing every day, finishing the book *Writing Tools,* researching your first ten publications, starting your own blog, and pitching the publications you researched.

For your dreams? You'll just have to sit down for your monthly planning session and see. Set a recurring reminder in your phone once a month to reflect on your yearly goals and craft your monthly planner. Break your monthly goals into the same format as your yearly ones: career, health/fitness, fun/self-love, learning, financial, and giving goals.

Make a Weekly Action Plan Every Sunday

Now that you have a monthly strategy of how you'll tackle your yearly goals, you're ready to break those goals into weekly action plans. This is where you'll convert every monthly goal that isn't already an action step into one you can look at in the morning and say, "I'm going to do THAT!"

Take our fictitious *NYT* yearly goal, for instance, with the "build a website" monthly goal. Building a website is time-consuming and can't happen in one swoop. So you reflect on that big goal and see how you can break it down.

(This is called strategizing. And the more you do it, the better you get.) For week one of month one, that might look like this:

- Draft copy for "about me," contact, and homepages.
- Research your favorite websites and take notes on how you want your site to look.

- Edit ten of your best articles for blog page.

Week two might involve reading a book/watching video tutorials on building a WordPress website and picking a theme—if you're going to do it yourself. Or if you're paying for a site, you'd talk to five developers, compare prices/products, then select one for the job.

You're going to use the same planning format as you've done with your monthly planner: career, fun/self-love, etc., except that you'll add one new section, "Daily Non-Negotiables." That goals section is simply for the things you have to do every single day to be your best. That could be writing an article per day, doing a specified amount of exercise, reading the relevant books, etc.

Once you've concluded your weekly planning session, you'll know every single action you're going to take this week to be a balanced, purposeful, and successful human. That means you don't have to worry about whether you're doing enough anymore or have anxiety about what you should plan in a day because it's all there in your weekly action plan.

Write Out Your Top Goals in a Daily Planner

Once you've come up with a monthly strategy and weekly action plan, you're already in the top 5 percent of planners in the world. Seriously. Nobody does this stuff, and it's so easy! But as soon as you start using your weekly action plan as a reference for your daily plan, you're unstoppable.

All you have to do is flip your planner back to your weekly action plan, see what five or so goals you could kick butt at today, and write those goals down in a new daily planning page. This takes all of two minutes.

Just make sure to include checkboxes next to each goal, and set reminders for the critical ones—and you're officially a planning expert. But more than that, you'll consistently accomplish the long-term habits that bring you the health, happiness, wealth, and purpose you've been dreaming about.

CHAPTER EIGHT

Self Development

Earl Nightingale

In the last chapter, you read motivational author Earl Nightingale's take on overcoming adversity. He was no stranger to hard times, having been born at the dawn of the Great Depression. For a short time, Nightingale and his single mother had to live in a tent city after his father abandoned them. Later, he served in the U.S. Marine Corps and was on the USS Arizona when it was attacked at Pearl Harbor. He was only one of a handful of Marines who survived the catastrophic attack. He later went on to a successful radio career, and his broadcast program "Our Changing World" became the most syndicated radio show in history.

In 1960, he founded the Nightingale-Conant Corp. with Lloyd Conant, which remains one of the biggest sellers of motivational content. He died in 1989.

Here, in this essay, Nightingale discusses the role of self-development in a successful life and career.

◈ ◈ ◈

COLLECT YOUR ROCKS WISELY

You can tell what you value most highly by assessing your past decisions, by seeing what you have, in fact, achieved. What you possess, what you place importance upon, what you felt has been worth striving for, what you wish to be, what you value most highly. When we look at ourselves in the light of our originality and realize we still cling to vestigial fears no longer needed, as useless as the disappearing limbs of the whale, as we stand in the arch of our experience and see the untraveled world before us, and despite the nagging doubts that must plague us from time to time, I think we have to agree with Tennyson's Ulysses, and say, "Come, my friends. 'Tis not too late to seek a newer world."

I got my inspiration for this piece when I reread one of the "Markets of Change" series which appeared in 1970 in *Kaiser News*, published by Kaiser Aluminum and Chemical Corp. and edited by Don Faben. That was one of the finest series of publications I've ever had the joy of reading, and I feel genuinely sorry for any person who did not have the opportunity to read them, and the artwork and the typography were as great as the original scholarly writing. The piece begins like this:

> *Once upon a time, there evolved upon this planet an organism that was ill-suited for survival. It could not run fast enough to escape its enemies. If caught, its teeth and claws were small protection. It was too big to hide under a leaf and too weak to burrow deeply into the ground. To survive,*

it took refuge in caves, where a fire at the entrance kept predators at bay. If the fire ran out of fuel, this creature could hurl rocks, and thus drive all but the most determined enemies away. Its security was measured by the amount of firewood it could accumulate and the number of rocks it could gather and store in the cave against the terrors of the night.

All other creatures grew bigger teeth or learned to run faster. Alone among all the creatures on Earth, the one we're describing turned to things for its survival. This was, in the end, to make all the difference. After a while, this creature learned to cultivate some edible plants to supplement the food it could get by gathering and hunting. Growing food was at best uncertain and in any event depended on the seasons, which could not be controlled. And the creature began to store its surplus foods. His security against the vagaries of nature was measured by how much he could grow and how much he could store. Well-being was measured quantitatively: the more, the better. From the very beginning, he was motivated by fear: fear of pain, fear of death, fear that there wouldn't be enough. In time, these creature's activities produced so much that it became more convenient to represent the accumulation of things with other things, smaller and easier to carry, or to exchange.

These symbols, although intrinsically of no value, assumed the same value as things, and men, or at least most men, became engaged in the acquisition and accumulation of the symbols of things. They did this even when they no longer had any need for them. The symbols were the surrogates for the rocks piled in the cave against the coming of the night. Now, think of this system as being reinforced over and over, through hundreds of generations and thousands of years, through social approval, ritualization, and acculturation.

That there was something basically wrong with this way of life may be exemplified by the fact that those who refused to subscribe to the accumulation and storage of things, Christ, Mohammed, and Buddha, became the founders of the world's great religions. Well, the idea is not to stop collecting our rocks entirely, especially if we have families to think about, now and in the future. The idea is to collect our rocks wisely, or in these days, just collect a few.

I attended a conference recently, where one of the excellent speakers pointed out that 96 percent of the American people fail to achieve financial independence. The reasons for the virtual total state of impecuniousness rampant in the world's richest country are four. One, the high cost of living. That is, price and wage spirals, inflation. Two, the high cost of living high. Consumerism and a credit card society and philosophy where people in the millions are searching frantically for things to buy, instead of putting the same money to work in income-producing property and investments. Three, high taxes and multiple taxes, and taxes on top of taxes. Taxes that make our real take-home income look like a sheared sheepdog.

A family finds it's earning $20,000 a year, after a raise in pay. The man and his wife are ecstatic. What they fail to realize is that the raise in pay has only kept pace with the rising cost of living, but at the same time, the raise in pay has placed them in a new tax bracket. They're now paying more taxes on money, which does not constitute a raise in real pay at all. But they don't realize that, and they move to a larger house, basing their choice of home on the old established multiple of four times annual income. But they think their annual income is $20,000 a year when in actuality, it's more like $12,000. And they start living on $20,000 a year, and trying to pay for it with $12,000. And it's then they find themselves getting behind what's known as the power curve. They find themselves borrowing money this year to pay last year's income taxes, then find that they have to pay this year's taxes plus the amount they've borrowed, plus the amount it takes to live on their new, higher standard, which is based on an amount of money they're not really earning anyway. Add to this the higher cost of living, for

◈ ENTREPRENEUR TIP

Do you know your tax bracket? Really know it? With recent changes to the tax law, you might want to follow up with your CPA or tax professional to make sure you clearly understand how those changes affect you. Knowing where you stand can help you make better business decisions going forward. As Nightingale mentions, don't misunderstand your bracket and live above your means.

everything from schools and lawn tools to eggs and gasoline, and our new young executive with his Brooks Brothers suit finds that he's developed an entirely new capacity for sweating, and for lying with his eyes wide open in the dark.

So number one is the high cost of living, number two is the high cost of living high, number three is high taxes, and number four is the high cost of *leaving* [dying], which in all likelihood will bring you face-to-face, for the first time in your life, with the cost of probate and the wolves of the IRS with regard to estate taxes. At one time, we all lived in a large pasture in which we were free to frolic, work, eat, and reproduce. And then the government cut the pasture in half, with income taxes. Then it was cut in half again and again and again by added taxes. It's not too difficult to see why 96 percent of the American people wind up flat broke and disillusioned about how to play the "collect the rocks for the cave" game.

It's true that some people are able to collect the symbol of things, money, even when they no longer need it. But they constitute perhaps one-half of 1 percent of the population. And it's better to have a few more rocks than you need, since none of us knows for sure how long they are going to live and need them, than it is to run out of them entirely when we're 65 and still have 15 to 20 good years ahead of us.

Let me try to remember an example of how what seems to look good can be something entirely different in reality. Let's say you have $10,000 invested at 10 percent compounded—a very handsome rate of interest, you'll agree. That brings you a return of $1,000. But you're in the 50 percent tax bracket, which cuts that down to $500. Add state and local taxes, which take another 6 percent or 7 percent, and you've got $460 or something (and we're being very generous; the rate of inflation this past year was figured at 7 percent), well, when you get through, you had a net return on your 10 percent of $10,000 of—get this—minus 2.5 percent. What looked like a truly regal return on your money was in actuality putting you in the hole. That's why the majority of working people in our society have a negative cash flow: Earnings do not produce security. We need to put that $10,000 into a tax-deductible investment that will produce no current taxable income, that will produce tax free buildup and eventually, when you need it, a tax-favored payout, since it's capital gains. In addition, we need an orderly method of transferring our estate at death to an IRS-approved investment and trust arrangement.

But first, we need to find the income we need so that we can create a meaningful estate. And to do that, we must either augment our means or diminish our wants, as Ben Franklin suggested. We must live within our means, whatever those means happen to be. If we can theoretically afford to live in a $100,000 home, let's live in a $50,000 house and agree to apply a two-point common sense rule to everything we buy or want to buy. Whenever we find ourselves facing a buying situation, we test it against two questions: One, do I really need it? Is it necessary? Then two: Can I afford it? The second question should be based on an actual understanding of what our true income is, after taxes, after expenses, and after provision for our future.

I heard about a high-income doctor who faced imminent bankruptcy. He was deeply in debt, owed last year's taxes, and was living beyond his means. Working with his financial planner, in two years he was debt free and saving money the right way. It's seldom too late to get squared away, but we must guard against letting our living standard go up as our income goes up, because as a rule, it's not a real increase in income at all. It's just keeping pace with inflation and putting us in progressively higher income tax brackets.

Albert Camus wrote in his notebooks, "It is a kind of spiritual snobbery that makes people think they can be happy without money." And if you don't think he's right, try it sometime.

⚜ ENTREPRENEUR TIP

Think for a minute how Nightingale's outlook here can be updated for a modern business environment. How can your business serve its community beyond providing goods or services? The answer could be social entrepreneurship. By including a social justice element in your business through volunteerism, donations, or selling products/services with a social impact, you can still realize profits while leading the charge for greater socioeconomic parity in your community.

Ogden Nash wrote, "Certainly, there are lots of things in life that money won't buy, but it's very funny: Have you ever tried to buy them without money?"

What do those who are trying to help the poor and the disadvantaged want? They want and need money. They need federal and state money, but that money comes from hardworking people. It comes out of the money in the pocketbook, whether it's a person or a company; all of it comes from taxes. We need to build whole, new, clean communities and better schools; we need to tear down the rat-ridden, mind-grinding, spirit-killing human dumps that exist in our big cities and replace them with cleanliness and order. It can only be done with money and more money.

THE ROLE OF MONEY IN SOCIETY AND BUSINESS

G.B. Shaw wrote of the Seven Deadly Sins: food, clothing, heat, rent, taxes, respectability, and children. Nothing can lift those seven millstones from man's neck but money. And the spirit cannot soar until the millstones are lifted. You know, millions live under the weight of a constant pressure, are torn by a ridiculous ambivalence that there is somehow something wrong with money, that money is evil. That to think about money and plan how to earn more money, indeed, to earn a lot of money is, is wrong somehow.

G.B. Shaw also wrote, "Money is indeed the most important thing in the world, and all sound and successful personal and national morality should have this fact for its basis." Remember that, as Logan Piershall Smith put it, "There are few sorrows, however poignant, in which a good income is of no avail." The myth that there is something evil in money was put in the minds of the masses by those who had all the money. "Keep them poor and stupid and we'll stay rich," was the slogan of the rich in those days. Today, we know that the best thing that can happen to people, to all of the people, is a measure of affluence, a substantial, more than adequate income.

You know, Karl Marx's mother once said, "If Karl, instead of writing a lot about capital, made a lot of capital, it would have been much better." There was a mother who knew what she was talking about. If all we did was sit under a tree and meditate and pass wisdom along to passing strangers, or wander the country, teaching a better life with no spouses, children, mortgages, taxes, dogs, schools, medical bills, automobiles, clothing, food, transportation, and clubs to concern ourselves about, we wouldn't have to pile rocks in our cave. But most of us seem to want these things, despite their onerous cost, and so maybe it's a good idea to find ways of having them without sweating ourselves into an early grave.

C. Northcote Parkinson is the discoverer of Parkinson's Law, which states that work expands so as to fill the time available for its completion. There is a similar automatic growth that takes place in organizations. For instance, in the British Navy, when the number of ships began to decline, the number of people employed continued to grow. When the British Empire began to dissolve, the number of people employed to administer the affairs of the Empire continued to grow. To this day, the number is still rising, even though the Empire has disappeared. Someone predicted that if everything continues on course, by the year 2195, everyone in Britain will be working for the government. One of our large banks did some research and came to the conclusion that if the trend for the last ten years continues, everyone in America will be working for the government by the year 2049. Meanwhile, the concentration of economic power continues. Anthony Jay, in his book, *Corporation Men*, concludes, "It seems almost inevitable that well before the end of this century, most of the wealth of the Western world will be controlled by three to six hundred giant international corporations. The only argument now is about the exact number."

YOUR SELF-DEVELOPMENT

[Here, the author moves from a discussion about the role of money in relation to self-development to a more direct application.] The definition of *entrepreneur* is one who assumes the risk and management of business, an enterpriser. And I read in *Ethics*, the international journal of social, political, and legal philosophy published by the University of Chicago Press, in an article titled "Kierkegaard, the Self and Ethical Existence," by George J. Stack of the State University of New York, a quotation of Kierkegaard that should make us all stop and think. He said, "There is nothing of which every man is so afraid of as getting to know how enormously much he is capable of doing and becoming." And then Stack writes that one can refuse to seek self-knowledge, can live an unexamined life or call fall into moral indifference, but the life of such a being is not the life of a person, nor of an authentically existing individual." He then wrote, "Not to take up responsibility for one's self is to lose the possibility of being a self, and by coming to know the actual self, as far as this is possible, one accepts responsibility for what one has been, and one is now capable of deliberate choice. Choice integrates the various aspects of the self, unifies and consolidates the diverse, often contradictory tendencies of the potential self." In another place, Professor Stack writes, "One of the most primitive forms of self-alienation is manifested when an individual does what they want him to do, 'they' meaning significant others, dominant or influential others, even though it's something which he consciously does not want to do."

Perhaps we should hit those points in order. First, it's by finding ourselves that we can come to know how enormously much we're really capable of doing and becoming. It is not by acting a part, trying to live like other people, living a secondhand and derivative life that we come to know our real powers. It's by finding ourselves. It's by examining and exploring ourselves and taking full responsibility for ourselves. Not to take up responsibility for one's self, as Professor Stack writes, is to lose the possibility of being a self, and by coming to know the actual self, as far as this is possible, one accepts responsibility for what one has been, and one is now capable of deliberate choice. Choice integrates the various aspects of the self, unifies and consolidates the diverse, often contradictory tendencies in a potential self.

One of the most primitive forms of self-alienation, of cutting ourselves away from the real and powerful person we truly are, comes about when we do what "they" want us to do, even though it's something we consciously do not want to do. In another part of the article, Professor Stack writes about the importance of choice and says, "We do not deliberate about driving our car from one place to another, from our place of work to our home. We simply do it voluntarily." There are, however, specific moments when we're confronted with choices that we know will have important ramifications for our lives. A person may ask himself, 'Should I pursue this career or that? Should I live in accordance with ethical categories or not? Should I marry or not? Should I serve in combat in time of war, or should I be a conscientious objector? Should I believe in the existence of God or not?' There are some options which one encounters that are momentous options for ourselves. And the important thing is to choose."

Since this resoluteness is an affirmation of one's self, an expression of one's individuality, irresolution is either an incapacity to choose or an unwillingness to choose. What is lacking is serious or passionate concern. The great quotation by Emerson pops into my mind. He said, "What a new face courage puts on everything." It's by having the courage to make the decisions that represent our real gut choices, to take responsibility for our decisions and our lives, that we will find our true powers.

As Mumford writes, the great mass of comfortable, well-fed people of our civilization live lives of emotional apathy and mental torpor, lives of enfeebled desire, secondhand lives. He said, "The Greeks had a word for this pallid simulacrum of real existence. They called it Hades." I think it can be said that the great majority of people do not really live, as we like to think of that word, at all. They spend their lives as puppets, with the strings in the hands of "they." What "they" say, what "they" think, how "they" live.

George Stack reminds us that Socrates held that "it is by no means necessary that everyone become a man," and Kierkegaard held "it is by no means necessary or inevitable that one become a person or an integral self." The act of choosing is not only individuating, but it's an act whereby the individual both expresses and attains freedom. The primitive freedom an individual has is the freedom for possibility. Before William James, Kierkegaard insisted that "only in a world in which there is possibility is freedom itself possible."

FINDING PERSONAL FREEDOM

Freedom is not, as it was for Spinoza, the recognition of necessity, but it is manifested in and made possible by the appropriation of necessity and possibility. Human freedom is not given as such, except as a possibility that may be actualized. It is the finite freedom of a person who is shaped and influenced by some circumstances that are outside his power. Man is determined in his being, but determining in his becoming. Choosing one's self as determined is a condition for the possibility of realizing one's self as free for possibilities positive for one's self, and not to act on a possibility is to run the risk of losing that possibility. And I've long been of the opinion that trying to play it too safely is about the best way in the world to remove most of all possibility from our lives and end by missing the boat, and by missing ourselves and our powers.

Dr. Frederick S. Perls agreed with this idea, too. His book, *Gestalt Therapy Verbatim*, is one of the most charming, educating, and refreshing books I've read in a long time. I've become a fan of gestalt therapy [which focuses on personal responsibility and experience in the present moment], and as he points out in the frontispiece: "To suffer one's death and to be reborn is not easy." I think we do this when we shrug off the phony life imposed upon us by others and the environment as much as we can and take responsibility for ourselves and our future. The meditation in *Gestalt Therapy* is great; it goes like this: "I do my thing, and you do your thing. I am not in this world to live up to your expectations, and you are not in this world to live up to mine. You are you and I am I. And if, by chance, we find each other, it's beautiful. If not, it can't be helped."

The great Robert Louis Stevenson has long been one of my favorites, not just as a great writer, but as a man as well. Plagued by a frail body and poor health, destined to die at just 44 years of age, he put more living, more travel, and more work and talent into his short time here on Earth than a million so-called average men. The author of *Treasure Island, Kidnapped!* and *Dr. Jekyll and Mr. Hyde*, Stevenson once wrote in a small essay:

Courage and intelligence are the two qualities best worth a good man's cultivation. So it is the first part of intelligence to recognize our precarious estate in life, and the first part of courage to be not at all abashed by the fact. A frank and somewhat headlong carriage, not looking too anxiously before, not dallying in maudlin regret over the past, stamps the man who is well-armored for this world. And not only well-armored for himself, but a good friend and a good citizen, to boot. We do not go to cowards for tender dealings. There is nothing so cruel as panic. The man who has least fear for his own carcass has most time to consider others. So soon as prudence has begun to show up in the brain like a dismal fungus, it finds its first expression in the paralysis of generous acts. The victim begins to shrink spiritually. He develops a fancy for parlors with a

regulated temperature. The care of one important body and soul becomes
so engrossing that all the noises of the outer world begin to come thin and
faint into the parlor with the regulated temperature.

Stevenson makes some important points in those few words, don't
you think? The first and most important being that the two qualities best
worth a good man or woman's cultivation are courage and intelligence,
and that it's the first part of intelligence to recognize our very precarious
estate in life, and thus not play it too safely. There's no way to win that
game. Tiptoeing through life won't change the final outcome. As soon as
too much prudence begins to show up in the brain, like a dismal fungus, it
finds its first expression in a paralysis of generous acts. The victim begins to
shrink, and so on. Some people worry so much about the future that they
fail entirely to enjoy today.

LET GO OF FEAR

The fear of life is the favorite disease of the 20th century. Too many people
are afraid of tomorrow. Their happiness is poisoned by a phantom. Many
are afraid of old age, forgetting that even if they should lose their bodily
vigor, weakness itself may minister to the development of the mind and
spirit. Instead of chagrin over the past and alarm over the future, suppose we
consider our opportunity? As Emerson put it, "Write it on your heart that
every day is the best day in the year. No man has earned anything rightly until
he knows that every day is Doomsday."

A small lesson from three great minds: Stevenson, Phelps, and Emerson.
Courage and intelligence are the two qualities best worth our cultivation,
and don't play it too safe. The man who has the least fear for his own carcass
has more time to consider others. There's a little green paperback book
entitled *The Gospel of Emerson*. It's a book which, if you'll read it quietly and
thoughtfully, will bring a marvelous new peace and understanding. Emerson
was one of the truly gifted intellectual giants of all time. He saw things with
a wonderful clarity, through layers of the obvious and commonplace, to the
kernel of truth that lay within.

In reading the little book on Emerson, I came across this line hidden
down at the end of a paragraph: "People wish to be settled; only as far as they

are unsettled is there any hope for them." You know, that takes some thinking to understand, but it's one of those statements we know intuitively to be true. Even though we strive to become settled and seek the mirage of security, we know that we do our best, think our best, accomplish most, and will certainly live more fully when we're unsettled. As Emerson put it: "Only as far as they are unsettled is there any hope for them." In other words, few of us know what's good for us. There's a security of a kind available to each of us, more than we require, really, but it's inside, not outside. It's to be found in the development of ourselves as creative, productive beings, loving and thinking persons, that real security is to be found. It cannot be outside of us. If we're not secure as persons, we will only stew and worry about any other sort of security, or being settled. And so we usually strive hardest for chimera, and that's what often brings so much disillusionment in later life, when people begin to sit around and stare at each other and wonder what they've been up to. Being settled is all right for cows and goldfish, I suppose, although I'm not at all sure about that, but being settled doesn't seem to work at all with human beings. They get nervous and querulous, start snapping at each other. They also get fat and sloppy and turn inward upon themselves and get unhappy expressions on their faces when they've been settled for very long. They find that the very thing for which they've striven for so long is not what they want at all. It's the fun of the journey, but usually in belated retrospect, that really matters. It's while they're striving that they reach their heights. Only as far as they are unsettled is there any hope for them.

⚜ ENTREPRENEUR TIP

What's getting in the way of feeling "settled" with yourself and your success journey? It just might be imposter syndrome, the belief that you are somehow not worthy of your success or that you are fooling everyone. How do you get past it? Start by incorporating some affirmative habits into your daily routine. Do some positive self-talk in the mirror each morning. Or you can list two to three things that you have accomplished each day (or month, or year) so you can see the results of your efforts. Give yourself room to fail and recognize that you are where you're meant to be.

BE SERVICE-MINDED

Living on the edge, striving toward goals still fairly distant, brings out the best or the very worst in people. If they're wise, it brings out the best, if they're ignorant, it can bring out the worst. But being settled, having it made, as we say, seldom brings with it much enthusiasm. Emerson also said, "Nothing great was ever achieved without enthusiasm, and we are most enthusiastic when we are as yet unsettled." There are many paradoxes in life, and one is that while people wish to be settled, it is only as far as they are unsettled that there's any hope for them.

Attached to the telephone of a young executive of my acquaintance is a small sign that reads, "God give me the wisdom to be as smart as my customers." There is a ton of good sense and worlds of growth opportunity lurking in that small, pithy comment. If there's one attitude common among those who serve the buying public, it's often an attitude which says, "OK, dummy, what'll it be?" It's an attitude which makes the mistake of assuming that because I work in this business, I know all there is to know about it, while the customer doesn't know anything about it at all. Because of that situation, I am infinitely wise, while the customer I now see approaching is infinitely stupid.

Now, I don't mean to say that all who serve the public feel that way by any means. A good percentage of them are great and a joy to do business with, and we remember them and go back to them whenever we can. And I don't mean to pick on the salespeople or the service people, particularly. The boss is the one who frequently makes the mistake of underestimating the public, or assumes most people are as dumb as they are. Some time back, I was checking into a motel and soon, I was back at the desk, asking them to make reservations for me somewhere else. The desk clerk asked me what was wrong, and I simply said, "Your motel isn't good enough." Traveling is tough enough without having to stay in a small, dirty room with an indifferent shower that goes from scalding hot one minute to ice cold the next, with the tile and plaster falling off the walls and ceiling. They underestimate the customer, or feel they have a lock on business, whether the customer likes it or not. The primary function of any organization is to help people enjoy a more meaningful existence.

That little legend ought to be cast in bronze and put every place in a business firm. The primary function of any organization is to help people enjoy a more meaningful existence. Now, if it isn't meeting that qualification, the people in it should get into something else. The definition of genius is to think in unhabitual ways. A day should never pass in which people in business do not ask themselves, "How can we do a better job of serving our customers?" But the number of businesspeople who ask themselves that question every day could fit easily into the back seat of a Volkswagen. Instead of concentrating on the cash register, if they would concentrate more on serving the customer, the cash register would take care of itself.

We shouldn't get our causes and effect mixed up. By making our product or service right, all else will fall into place. It's just a matter of time and perseverance. But we should never underestimate the customer and his natural desire for quality, for value for his time and money. The businesspeople who have heeded that kind of thinking have prospered. Anyway, it's a good idea, that little sign: "God give me the wisdom to be as smart as my customers." And we might add: "And to serve them as I enjoy being served when positions are reversed." And that business of thinking in unhabitual ways can also bring a fresh, clean breath of renewal into a business.

BRING YOUR IDEAS TO LIFE

Imagination, you know, is everything. Wilfred A. Peterson, author of "The Art of Living in the World Today," writing in *Science of Mind* magazine sometime back, quoted Felix Adler, who once said, "I am grateful for the idea that has used me." And Peterson went on to say, "There are millions of great ideas in the world waiting for men and women to use them." For people to dedicate their minds, hearts, spirits, eyes, ears, hands, arms, and legs to putting those ideas into action. There's no lack of ideas waiting to be used, there's only a lack of people willing to use them. The idea of the electric light used Edison. The idea of flying the Atlantic used Lindbergh, the idea of saving the Union used Lincoln. The idea of building a hospital in Africa used Schweitzer. The idea of writing *Uncle Tom's Cabin* used Harriet Beecher Stowe. Ideas use people when people work for those ideas, when people are dominated by those ideas and make them a part of themselves. The ideas need not be world-shaking; ideas may be limited and yet meaningful. The idea of a new school in the community, the idea of a new church. There are ideas for thousands of projects that will contribute in large or small measure to mankind. Ideas, of themselves, do nothing. Used by men, they can do anything.

The idea of peace is a great idea, perhaps the very greatest that people should open themselves to and be used by. The idea of war has been used by man for far too long a time. It's sent millions marching to their death, destroyed cities, wrecked the world. We need to be gripped by the idea of peace. We should get it into our hearts, into our blood streams, into our bones, and make it a part of ourselves. It's been waiting around for a long time for men to use.

The supply of great ideas is inexhaustible. Let a great idea use you. Stand up for it, work for it, teach it, sell it, crusade for it. Help a great idea to become a reality through you. Well, I think that's a great little piece, because it should make clear to those who are searching for something to do, some kind of work to get into, a way in which they can not only find something to do but at the same time be swept up and along by an idea that's bigger than they are. Find an idea you think is interesting and exciting and jump into it with both feet, head, hands, and heart. Let a great idea use you. A great idea might be to build and operate the best business of its kind. Marshall Field had that idea. Great restaurants, hardware stores, supermarkets, any sort of business. You don't have to make a great invention or win the Nobel Peace Prize. A business motivated by a great idea will succeed out of all proportion to a business operating only for profit. So will a career in anything: selling,

◈ ENTREPRENEUR TIP

Ready to bring your next "great idea" to life? Have a blue-sky meeting with your team. Put your new idea in front of the team and have everyone in the room envision all the things they can do to bring that big, new idea to fruition. In a blue-sky meeting there are no bad ideas—only possibilities. At the end of your session, choose the top five tasks/concepts/approaches that seem most viable and start drafting your master plan.

law, medicine, farming. A person moved by an idea that's bigger than they are can move a lot of mountains during their lifetime. A great idea is like a broad, swift river: Once you've found the one you want, all you have to do is jump in and start swimming. It'll carry you along much faster than you could have traveled otherwise.

CHOOSE YOUR PATH

In the world of today, it seems that each of us needs to choose between one of three courses: recognizing that we are undergoing changes unprecedented in human history, we can choose to escape from the world, to help build a better world, or to just hang on for dear life and hope that the whole thing doesn't fly apart during our lifetimes. How about you?

We're in a whole new ball game, and it takes some shifting of gears. We've found, for example, that affluence does not satisfy wants; it simply creates new ones, more voracious, more difficult to satisfy than the old ones. Utopia involves the satisfaction of wants, but the wants of man are insatiable. Supply one and two rise to take its place. And man is the only creature so constituted. Satisfy the wants of an animal, and he'll drop off into a peaceful sleep, totally content. Not man. Satisfy man's wants, and his eyes bug out looking for new ones. That's one of the reasons there's no end in sight to the possible growth of business, which is, in many ways, good.

The same technology that created the monsters which terrify us now— overpopulation, pollution, wars, and crime—can contain them, ultimately do away with them entirely, I'm sure. Technology gives us what we want, and then it lets us see, as a New York University professor put it, that while dissatisfaction may be uncomfortable, the real disasters in life come from getting what we want. But only temporarily, during man's painful maturing process.

Of the three choices open to us (escape, reconstruction, or teeth gritting and hanging on), I think most of us want to help put things together in a better way. And one way each of us can do that is to strive for quality in whatever it is we do. Simplify our lives, cut down on the number of things we'll permit to engage our attention, and make sure they're of good quality. When you're building on quality, you're building long-term growth. If we refuse to let junk appear in our lives, it will disappear from our lives. If we refuse to buy things we think are priced too high, the prices will come down. We can make do with what we've got. If the homes in the new development all look exactly alike and there are no trees, let's not buy one. And let's not buy anything that has not been well constructed to last a long time. Let's carefully examine and check out things before we'll permit them to enter our lives. And most importantly of all, let's make sure that what we do is of the best quality possible.

The late Ernest Holmes wrote something we'd do well to remember every morning as we begin our day. He said:

> *Create or perish is the eternal mandate of nature. Be constructive or become frustrated is an equal demand. We do not all have to act or think alike, but each should give full reign to the urge within him to express his life. This thing called life is intimate to everyone, even as the law of cause and effect is available to all. Take your place, then, in the universe in which you live, having neither fear nor arrogance, but in the simplicity of faith, come to believe that you are one with the creative genius back of this vast array of ceaseless motion, this original flow of life. You are as much a part of it as the sun, the Earth, and the air. There's something in you telling you this, like a voice echoing from some mountaintop of inward vision, like a light whose origin no man has seen. Like an impulse welling up from an invisible source. Your mind is an outlet through which the creative intelligence of the universe seeks fulfillment.*

It's good, isn't it? And powerful. It reminds me of Emerson's great quote that says we should listen to the voice within. He wrote, "Create or perish, be constructive or become frustrated. We may dread the work that lies ahead of us tomorrow, but we should dread even more a time when we will have nothing at all to do tomorrow, when there's nothing for us to do. And so, let's create. Let's bring something new, something better because of us, to our work, which is what creation is all about."

There are all kinds of people in the world. There are the bizarre, the decadent, the bored, the disenchanted. There are the mindless hedonists, the shallow seekers of distraction. There are the grim cynics to whom nothing is nor can be good or meaningful. But the happiest people on Earth are those who, out of themselves, create conditions beneficial to those it has been given them to serve. They create happy homes, good meals, education, better health, enjoyment, humor, new buildings, products, services, a better job, a helping hand, better government. Wherever they are, things are better for them having been born. They bring something of themselves to their work, something that makes it better. They are constructive, they are the builders of the world. They listen to the iron string that vibrates deep within them, of which Emerson spoke.

Ernest Holmes went on to say, "The greatest gift life could have made to you is yourself." You are a spontaneous, self-choosing center in life, in the great drama of being, the great joy of becoming, the certainty of eternal expansion. You could not ask for more, and more could not have been given. You need not mold your life after another; trust yourself. Believe in your direct relationship with life, and you will not be disappointed. But do not wait. Today is the time to start. Right where you are is the place to begin.

❧ ENTREPRENEUR ACTION ITEM
Create Your Self-Development Mindset

The most fulfilling path to success and personal fulfillment comes through the pursuit of your own self-development, as Nightingale mentioned in the essay you just read. The radically successful and happy immerse themselves in self-development and a deep interest in life and relationships. Through self-exploration they remain openly curious and passionate about their self-education and improvement. They hold the belief that they can only learn if they are willing to risk themselves personally and professionally.

Through life's experiences, good and bad, you become able and ready to be proactive in all your efforts, challenges, and successes. You choose to no longer wait for success or happiness; you go out and make it happen. Making a commitment to your own development is the first step on the path to living your personal legend. Here are some important elements of a self-development mindset.

Sense of Self

Self-improvement begins with a keen awareness of who you are, your values, beliefs, and the larger purpose you wish to pursue. True satisfaction can only manifest from chasing your own dreams. Life, people, and business can be hard and insensitive, so remind yourself that you are more than the sum total of other people's opinions and continue pursuing what is meaningful to you.

The experiences you have in life can only have true meaning when you seek to understand them. To become a pristine student of life is to always remain teachable-ready. Examine how each experience life brings can be used for greater self-knowledge and better decisions going forward. As you gain a more solid sense of who you are, you become ready to start planning, designing, and pursuing your goals and objectives.

Sense of Curiosity

To live successfully, be endlessly curious about all the possibilities your future holds. It is important to have an unquenchable thirst for your advancement and for adventure. Curiosity inspires you to push through the unusually painful trials and errors in your life and business. This type of resiliency is an acquired self-discipline that teaches you to cast your fears aside, bringing you the fullest experience of the adventures success can bring.

Curiosity creates a longing to know more and do more. It inspires that energy that makes it possible to see all situations as opportunities for your advancement. When you approach life and business with a sense of adventure, there is no situation, however limiting, physically or economically, which cannot be filled to the brim with the interest and curiosity of how it will all work out.

Without a sense of curiosity, it is impossible to grow.

Sense of Direction

The more you develop yourself, the more pristine you become in achieving what you want. This clarity makes decision making easier because having a direction improves your ability to prioritize. You know which objectives are important in the short term and which are necessary for your long term. With a sense of direction, you become focused and effective.

There is nothing more organizing to an effort than being focused. Direction provides commitment. It is difficult to commit to something that has no foreseeable future or path. If you are filled with doubt and a lack of clarity, there is no way to launch your ideas. Self-development gives you direction, and thereby, the commitment to achieve your ends.

Sense of Follow-Through

Knowing what you want to achieve makes it easier for you to see the benefits of taking action. Even when the tasks at hand are not enjoyable, seeing the benefit of following through on them will make it easier to motivate yourself into taking the necessary actions to achieve your goals. There is a lot of truth in the saying "Where there's a will, there's a way."

When you are committed to personal development, you always find a way to develop the necessary will. Your idea of success and the vision of what that will look like is where you grab your incentive to always follow through.

Sense of Urgency

A sense of urgency drives inspiration. Urgency creates the mindset to work as if your life depends on it, especially if you have fewer resources than others. When you are the underdog, you will dig deep inside yourself for the advances you need to thrive.

Urgency causes you to activate quickly when making decisions. You get out of your routine and do something different. It motivates you to get results quickly and efficiently, but it does not eliminate assessment. If you want to produce results faster, you must assess what is and what is not working, then eliminate the efforts that have been identified as wasteful. Keep in mind it is easier to steer a moving object, so if you realize you have made a poor decision, a sense of urgency allows you to adjust. If you wait too long, you miss opportunities and chances.

Sense of Resiliency

There will be tough times in life and business. When tough times occur, you need the skills and attributes to deal effectively with them. Personal development cannot prevent all bad things from occurring, but it helps you deal with obstacles as they surface.

Resiliency teaches you never to view any challenge as the end of the world. Resiliency allows you the patience, awareness, and fortitude to continue moving forward, even if that means completely changing course.

Self-development deepens your maturity to trust that everything happens for reasons that can only be in line with your best interest. With this type of mindset, there is no obstacle that will hold you back. You will have greater confidence, pliability, and the personal and interpersonal skills to cope with any obstacle you face to climb up the ladder of success.

Sense of Connectedness

Relationships can be double-edged swords. They either lift you up or drag you down. They either bring you closer to your goals or push you further away. When you improve your personal development, you are better able to see which relationships and partnerships are worth investing in and which you need to cut loose. This type of self-awareness gives you the skills to make the best of the relationships that have a positive impact on your life, your business, and your overall success.

If you aren't learning, then you aren't living. Make the commitment to invest in your greatest resource—you. Many people are put off by personal development because it's viewed as a weakness or something that shows you do not already possess the skills necessary for success. If you assume you already have it all, you will not be happy or successful. The greatest achievers in life and business know the key to success is their ability to manage themselves in a variety of situations. That ability comes through personal development.

CHAPTER NINE

Action Plan for Success: Your Psychological Needs

Dr. Lacy Hall

D r. Lacy Hall (1934–2014) led an accomplished life. He received his master's degree in philosophy from Duke University and his Ph.D. in psychology from the University of North Carolina. He served as a professor at a number of American universities. A prolific writer and lecturer, he specialized in testing and analyzing personality traits and developing measures of self-assessment. In addition to his years of educational work at universities, he was a director of counseling for the Peace Corps, director for employment counseling for the State of North Carolina and director of testing for the U.S. Armed Services.

The following "Action Plan for Success" provides guidance on how you can assess your capabilities and interests and use this knowledge to set and achieve your goals.

❖ ❖ ❖

IDENTIFY YOUR NEEDS

We all have needs. We are all very much aware of the various physical needs that we face. For example, if we do not get enough sleep or do not get enough to eat, we become aware that our physical-needs satisfaction is being neglected, and we can decide what has to be done to correct it.

So in the same way we want to satisfy our physical needs, we look for the satisfaction of psychological needs; we respond to others and to ourselves psychologically. There are certain basic psychological needs such as a need to be loved, to be recognized, and so forth, that are important for you to be aware of in this process towards your successful future.

Abraham Maslow has done an outstanding job in his observation on the fulfillment of needs in our lives and how we respond to these needs. He came to his awareness as he worked with those people who were considered to be very successful and had reached some fulfillment or self-actualization in their lives as he identified it. He wanted to identify those characteristics used in their lives that made them function as successful persons. As a result of this, Maslow developed a concept that there is a hierarchy of needs in all of our lives.

> ❖ **ENTREPRENEUR TIP**
>
> Take a moment to make a list of what you think your basic needs are. How do you think they differ from those of someone in another region, another state, or even another continent?

This hierarchy starts off with the very basic need of staying alive. This includes having enough to eat and drink, avoiding bodily harm, and having adequate shelter.

Now the interesting thing is that to many of us in our land these days, these very basic needs have not been a real challenge. We have taken them for granted. But to others, these have been and continue to be an ongoing challenge. There are people in developing countries, for example. They're not always sure that they are going to stay alive or have enough to eat and drink. Thus, Maslow is saying that before we try to help a person become self-actualized, which is at the top of your list, we must first see that these very basic needs are satisfied in their life.

However, for many, these basic needs have not been changed and therefore are not important to you. But what is important to you is that you are able to live a satisfying and fulfilling life and that your needs (either staying alive or doing what you want to do) are met and placed in their proper perspective. The challenge as we have found it, is that most of us have tried by hit or miss to determine what these needs are.

There is a systematic way to determine what needs have been fulfilled and what have not been fulfilled in your life. Thus, let's change your attitude about the fulfilling of your needs. We are not going to explore the negative past as we mentioned. The negative past does not have to be explored in order to change the present or to alter the future. Thus, we want to look at the positive or the helpful side of your needs and your life.

CREATE A NEEDS INVENTORY

Look at those needs that have been fulfilled as you have been fulfilled. Select eight different experiences, each illustrating an experience where things worked together or have been fulfilled, where you thought that at that

---

⚜ ENTREPRENEUR TIP

Take a moment to list the seminal experiences that have made you who you are as an entrepreneur. What are your successes? Do you see a pattern in them?

---

moment and through that experience that life is the way it should be, and it was a very wonderful and meaningful time for you.

Now, by using this definition as just suggested, this could mean many things to many different people. We are not trying to say that this meaningfulness or being fulfilled at a moment [in time] is the same for everyone. Your feelings are similar, but the events producing the feelings will be very different for each person. At this point, just think about the experiences that have happened in your life, that helped you to feel that all was well with the world, and that this was a wonderful day or a wonderful experience or series of experiences. Be as specific as you can and list these in eight columns on a sheet of paper or in a journal.

For example, we suggest that you list a very specific event, rather than something that's too general such as a family or job. All of us have to be honest—we may have had families that haven't been as fulfilling or as wonderful as others. But parts of them have and we have to look at the good side of some of these things. So now, let's pick a specific event in your life when you had a very fulfilling and rewarding experience. For example, were you on a specific type of trip? What happened on that trip? Were you on a picnic or is it a time when you were seated around the Christmas tree and having a discussion with your family? Now take that specific event; for example, the day you sat by the Christmas tree and talked about meaningful things with your family. Why was this particular event that you have selected meaningful or fulfilling to you?

Now, identify the needs that are important to you, and to write them down on the left hand side of the page. We suggest that the first two be "I was doing what I wanted to do," and "I was doing things the way they should be done." because these are critical needs for many people. You should select your own most important needs, however, and list them in this column. List as many as you believe are important to your success and happiness.

After you have entered an experience at the top of the first column, go down the left side and ask yourself: Was sitting about the Christmas tree, this particular experience, meaningful to me because it was doing what I wanted to do? If so, then place a check in the column. Was it doing things the way I thought they should be done? Then check. In other words, check off each of the statements that have helped you to decide if this was a meaningful experience in explaining it to you.

Now it could be that as you've gone down this first column, you would have checked five or six items. Then, while you are still reflecting on this first column, review these items that you have checked. Decide which seem to be the most important to you and put a circle around that one check. Then go to the second column and repeat the same process with a new experience that you have listed at the top.

Take a random sample of experiences from your family life, your business life, from association with friends, recreation, and so forth so that you could get a feeling of life in general for you.

Now as you go through the same process with each experience, ask yourself each of the questions you've created and circle the most important mark in each column. When you have finished the eight columns, you will have a composite of your psychological needs. You are saying that when these eight representative events have happened in your life, you have felt wonderfully together and fulfilled, that these are the needs that were fulfilled and which now help you to explain why these events were important to you.

TAKE ACTIONS THAT HONOR YOUR NEEDS

Hey, you have taken a wonderful first step. You are now saying that when you have been fulfilled, there are some needs that have made this possible. It could be that you were able to do what you wanted to do or you were able to learn some new things. But this is very important as a contribution that you have now made to yourself, because you are saying that when you have been successful, these are the psychological needs that have helped to explain how or why you have been successful. This means that as you look towards planning your future success, you would want to make sure that these are a part of your plan.

For example, if you like to do things the way you want to do them or if you want to learn new things or if you want to use skill and know-how, certainly as you look to planning your future success, you want to make sure that these are included in your activities.

Don't get yourself trapped in a situation where you can't learn new things if you're saying that every time you looked at yourself being fulfilled in the past, it was because you had learned something new. Don't get yourself into a position where you routinely go through the same thing day after day without learning something new and then you can't explain your boredom. If this is the case, you can now look and say, *I can now see that I haven't been learning anything new; no wonder I'm upset.*

Connect Your Strengths and Needs

Now, take the four or five needs from your list and write them on a new page. Add your list of needs to that page as well. Then, take some time to reflect on your personal strengths. Select five or six strengths that you feel are important to your functioning as a total person. As you look at the two columns of strengths and needs, study possible ways of combining your strengths and your needs so that you can now write a definition of success for yourself. In other words, you can say, "I am successful when I use these strengths and when I meet these needs." Now this isn't always easy; perhaps you have never thought of yourself in this way, but combine these two very important facets of your life; and you are saying at the present time, in the present state of growth, "I feel successful when I am able to use these strengths and to meet these needs."

Now why is this important? It is important because by using these strengths and meeting these needs, you have now established where you are as of *now*. Remember, we talked about how in order to get to where you want to be, you must decide where you are right now. You are saying what your definition of success is and you've written it out. Now it may be that you may not like the way this definition reads. This is a definition that has come out of what you have said your strengths are and what you have shared your needs are. And whether you like this or not, the important thing to understand is that you can do something about it. In light of what we have now looked at in our personal definition of success, let's do something about it, either to reinforce it or to challenge ourselves to change it towards the future in the way we want to be successful.

Set Goals

Now this is where we set goals. A goal is deciding what you are going to accomplish today, tomorrow, next year, or maybe even five years from now.

The goal is a decision on your part of an accomplishment or an achievement that you want to have completed and by a certain date. Thus, you are now saying, "In light of my definition of success, here is what I want to do to be a better salesperson, to become president of my company, to be a better husband or wife; this is my goal."

Once you have decided what your definition of success is, then you can begin to decide which goals you want to pursue. Now using this definition of success, you may want to change a goal. If it means changing yourself, your goal will help you make that decision as to the type of change you would like to make.

Now, one suggestion. Remember: Don't keep the goals too general; be as specific as you can. Is your goal conceivable, believable, achievable, controllable, measurable, desirable, stated with no alternatives, or growth-facilitating? Perhaps one thing you need to do is to reinforce something that you learned about yourself. To reinforce it is to make it stronger. So, you would want to set a goal to reinforce something about your definition of success or your strengths or your needs or some action.

Next, you may want to set a second goal; a goal to challenge the future, to enlarge the parameters of your life, or to open up new directions and new vistas for you. This would be a goal of new growth potentials in your life. Perhaps you want to explore some new type of marketing, a new type of selling, or whatever it might be. Your second goal might be to move in a new direction or redefining success or redirecting your life towards this new successful future that you are clarifying right now.

● ENTREPRENEUR TIP

As you set your goals, remember to keep them SMART: specific, measurable, achievable, relevant, and time-bound.

The average person in setting their goal plays games with himself or herself. So, you need to have someone help you in your goal-setting process. That someone then becomes a part of your support system. Share this first goal with a friend, a co-worker, or a relative. Tell that person when you would like to see this first goal completed, maybe in several weeks; how you would like to tell them about this [phone, text, email] and when you will share this information.

Now, why do you need this? Well, three basic reasons: First, this process helps you to clarify your goals in order to explain to yourself and to someone else. You can think more clearly about what it is you want to do. Next, when you select someone and say, "I would like to share a goal with you," that usually makes that person feel good because you thought enough of them to be invited into the goal-setting process. Next, it gives you that added incentive because you have shared this with them, you don't want to disappoint them. So, next, you will be thinking about when you can share the good news [that you've reached your goal]. There is a certain excitement on your part in preparing a report of good news to share with someone else, which makes you even more excited about getting the goal accomplished. And in that way, you are helping yourself by planning these activities, sharing them with others, and helping others to become a part of the excitement of the change in your development towards your successful future.

INSIGHTS FROM W. CLEMENT STONE ON GOALS, SUCCESS, AND HOW TO THINK

I feel healthy. I feel happy. I feel terrific. Every living person has one thing in common, regardless of the continent on which he is born and that includes women, as well as men, and it includes children. It's a machine, a brain, and a nervous system from which the mechanical computer was designed. And we've spent millions and millions and billions of dollars over the years, throughout the world, training people how to use computers, design programs, and build machines, but there isn't one of you that was taught how to use your brain and nervous system, the human computer.

When it comes to extracting the principles, [you have] the power within—I'm referring to passions, emotions, tendencies, moods, feelings— how to form desirable habits at will; how to eliminate undesirable habits at will; how to set goals; how to set high goals; and most importantly, how to achieve them.

Keep in mind that you have the powers of the mind that every other living person has in principle, but you may not know how to use it. You can learn how to use those powers so that you can achieve anything at all in life you desire. It doesn't make any difference what it is or how high it is, provided you are willing to pay the price to engage in thinking and planning a good use of your time. But you'll never do it unless you learn how, and that is why it would pay to read and then study and then understand the principles in such books as *Think and Grow Rich, Success Through a Positive Mental Attitude,* and *The Success System that Never Fails.* How many of you take the time to really study the important things of life about yourself, about how you can help your children, how you can help your community, how you can help your nation, or whatever it may be? You don't have to start big; you start with yourself. Learn how to use your own learning power. You've got the power, whether you recognize it or not.

Keep in mind the power of your mind, a God-given quality if you know how to use it. For example, my strength lies as a writer or as a sales manager in being able to share with others the how-to, what to do, and how to do it.

You are an important person and when you recognize that, and when you recognize that you have a brain and nervous system, and when you recognize that you are the product of heredity, environment, experience, your physical body, the use of your conscious mind and its impact on the subconscious, and your particular position in time and space, and something more (and this is important) including powers known and unknown and that you can harmonize with any one of them, for you are a mind with a body.

You may have attended great lectures and heard great speakers and nothing happened. The true test of how well a meeting works is that it results in action, not what you say, but what you do.

Think. Think in terms of what the meetings you attend [or books you read or podcasts you listen to] could mean to you. Are you the person you want to be? Think, concentrate. Are you the person your spouse, your children believe you to be? Think, think, think. Are you the person your loving parents prayed and hoped you would become? Think, think. Now change your line of thought and think in terms of your family. Are you as thoughtful, as loving, considerate as you were in the early days of your marriage? Think, be truthful with yourself. Think, think.

For those of you who have children, do you really love your children enough to learn how to discipline them intelligently? Think, think, think. Do you think enough of your family and yourself to learn how to use the greatest gift to man, namely the use of your brain and your nervous system? Think, think, think, think.

Now think of someone besides your immediate family. Are you as kind and thoughtful to your in-laws as you would want to have others be kind and thoughtful to you if conditions were reversed, because some day they may be reversed? Think, think, think.

ENTREPRENEUR TIP

You can apply this "think" process to colleagues and employees as well. How do you treat those with whom you work every day? How can you improve those relationships?

Now think in terms of someone besides those related to you. Is there anyone to whom you've been unkind when you should have been kind, some unfortunate person, someone who may have a displeasing personality? Think, think, think.

Now think in terms of this great nation of ours, the freedoms that you inherited, the opportunities that you have received. Think in terms of what you can do to pass onto your posterity these freedoms, these opportunities. And think in terms of what you have not done that you could have done. Think, think, think. And paraphrasing Edmund Burke, remember all that is essential for the triumph of evil is that good people like you do nothing. And then paraphrasing it, you can paraphrase that all is essential for the triumph of good is that good people like you get into action and do something about it. Think, think, think.

ENTREPRENEUR ACTION ITEM
This Is What It Takes to Spark Change in Your Life

Dr. Lacy Hall's take on goal-setting as it relates to advancing and improving your life is a practical, actionable way to put change in perspective. As we identify our needs and our goals, a clear picture of what we want the change in our lives to look like emerges. Change is recurrent in all aspects of life. Seasons change, technology changes, people change. Change is both necessary and unavoidable.

People often say that they want to change their job, their loved ones, even their bodies. But what sparks change in relationships, businesses, and life in general? As you begin each new year or new phase in your business, take time to see what needs to change in your life.

Change happens when a decision is made. Now is the time to create a framework for decisions that will initiate the action necessary to facilitate that change. Here are some thoughts to consider if you want to make a change in your life.

Be Willing to Change

We all know someone who wants to get in shape but keeps eating McDonald's and refuses to go to the gym. What about the friend who says they want a stable relationship but keeps dating troubled or emotionally unavailable people? If we want to make a change, we have to be willing to put in the work. Wanting to change is not enough. The pain of not changing has to be so severe you have no choice but to take action. Think about the consequences of not changing vs. the excuses you have not to.

Create Your Own Circumstances

We all have histories that make us who we are. Sometimes these stories serve as crutches when we allow them to prevent us from taking necessary action to make the changes we need in life. We can easily blame the market, our clients, or our spouses for not supporting our vision, but if we want to make a change we need to take ownership of our circumstances. In any situation, there are things we don't have control of, but there are also things we *can* control. To overcome your circumstances, you must identify opportunities to take responsibility and create the change.

Change Your Mindset to Change Your Life

Mindset dictates behavior. To create change we need to become aware of the actions we take daily and shift our perspective. Trying to do it overnight is the most common reason we fail to implement behavioral change. First, we need to change our mindset. We need to prove to ourselves that our current behavior doesn't serve us anymore, but there is a light at the end of the tunnel. Following that, change happens one day at a time. Eventually you will create a new pattern of behavior to replace the old one. When you strengthen your mindset, you empower yourself to take action.

Control Your Reactions

Statistics show that most people give up on their new year's resolution just 45 days into the year. Creating change is not easy. Like everything in life, you will experience setbacks. How you react to these setbacks determines your probability of success. Understand that it takes time, both in your business and in your life, to create meaningful change. Think of a time when you've encountered a challenge and reacted negatively. Did it help you solve the problem? See every failure as an opportunity to one up yourself.

Get Comfortable with Being Uncomfortable

Image a businessperson 25 years ago who, after first hearing about the internet, decided: "I will not change the way I worked all my life—the heck with the kids and their computers." That person probably is not in business today. You will achieve success if your drive to change is greater than the need to stay comfortable. Growth happens outside of your comfort zone.

Change Comes from Within

Believe that change is possible, and always keep that vision to propel you forward when times get tough. If you do not have that belief, and if you can't see the finish line, chances are that you are going to give up. Before expecting change from others, you have to spark and create the process of change and improve yourself first.

CHAPTER TEN

How to Get Control of Your Time and Your Life

Alan Lakein with an introduction by Og Mandino

W hat does it take to manage your life? Alan Lakein knows, and the answer is time. More to the point, the answer is time management. Lakein, a bestselling author who focuses on time management, has several books to his credit, including *How to Get Control of Your Time and Your Life*, which has sold well over 3 million copies. A graduate of Johns Hopkins and Harvard universities, Lakein obviously had to find a great way each day to tackle the stress. In this essay, he shares some of his best tips and tricks for getting better control of your time, which (not surprisingly) also affects your life in general.

Sales expert Og Mandino, bestselling author of *The Greatest Salesman in the World*, provides additional insight in his introduction below. His books have sold over 50 million copies in 25 languages.

❧ ❧ ❧

AN INTRODUCTION BY OG MANDINO

Time: What is it? Look in any anthology of great thoughts under the word *time,* and you will learn that just about every wise man in recorded history has made some sage commentary about time.

Arthur Brisbain said, "Regret for time wasted can become a power for good in the time that remains and the time that remains is time enough, if we will only stop the waste and the idle, useless regretting."

John Howe wrote, "What a folly to dread the thought of throwing away life at once, and yet have no regard to throwing it away by parcels and piecemeal."

On Queen Elizabeth's deathbed her last words were, "All my possessions for a moment of time."

I like what Benjamin Franklin said best of all: "Dost thou love life? Then do not squander time, for that is the stuff life is made of."

Like many other writers in the self-help field, I borrowed from Franklin and Queen Elizabeth in my book *The Greatest Salesman in the World,* when in Scroll 5 I wrote, "I will live this day as if it is my last. I have but one life, and life is naught but a measurement of time. When I waste one, I destroy the other. If I waste today, I destroy the last page of my life. Therefore, each hour of this day will I cherish for it can never return. It cannot be banked today to be withdrawn on the morrow, for who can trap the wind. Each minute of this day will I grasp with both hands and fondle with love for its value is beyond price. What dying man can purchase another breath though he willingly give all his gold? What price dare I place on the hours ahead? I will make them priceless! I will live this day as if it is my last."

Time is the only commodity in the world which is allocated equally to all: rich man, beggar, white man, black man, president, housewife, salesman, writer. All of us receive the same 24-hours a day. There are no favorites to that ticking clock.

Alan Lakein is a bona-fide expert in the planning of time. His clients include such corporate giants as American Tel & Tel, Bank of America, IBM, Lever Brothers, and Standard Oil of California.

I first saw this bright guy on the *Johnny Carson Show*. Soon after his book *How to Get Control of Your Time and Your Life* had been published. I listened and watched with fascination. Ten minutes later, I was convinced that I really didn't know as much about controlling my time as I thought I did. I bought Alan's book. It was tremendous. We began to correspond, and the ultimate result is this magic essay [originally produced as an audiobook] containing the essence of his techniques. But let me warn you: If you're waiting to hear any far-out, super sophisticated or complicated techniques to master time, you'll be disappointed.

What Alan Lakein shares with you instead are some simple, basic, but still little-known methods of controlling your time to get the most out of it. Learn them, and as Franklin said, you will be controlling far more than your time, you will be controlling your life.

LEARN HOW TO DO LESS

Many people on the way up allow their family and personal lives to be heavily impinged upon by work demands. Others are so achievement-oriented that they feel guilty taking time out for anything that's not in some way related to their work.

Horror stories abound of people who work so hard that they hardly ever see their families and who end up with ulcers and heart trouble. One study several years ago of successful and unsuccessful executives indicated that many men who ultimately fail had let their personal lives go by the wayside while keeping up with the rat race.

My experience with clients has convinced me that when executives find themselves on a treadmill, they tend to lose perspective on what's important. They spend time unnecessarily on secondary matters and let many important ones go undone. This often tends to be cumulative. The more overtime they put in, the more exhausted and less efficient they become. The answer is not to spend more hours on the project, but to work more effectively within the time allotted, to work smarter rather than harder.

I recall one architect who came to me suffering from too much work and not enough play. He had only recently recovered from a bleeding ulcer and again was working 60 hours a week. His complaint was that he never had time to see his wife and young children. I suggested that he take off at noon on Friday, and since summer was just beginning, take his family away to his favorite spot at Lake Tahoe. He rented a cabin where he and his family spent each weekend during the summer. Not surprisingly, he got to know his family again and his health improved. Since he knew that he couldn't make up for low productivity by long hours, he concentrated on getting the important things done in the time he had. He actually got more done than he ever had working 60 hours, even though he shaved more than 15 hours off that total. As a bonus, he got some of his most creative ideas while he was relaxing at the lake. So, his leisure time paid off handsomely. All he really lost by cutting back those 15 hours was the detailed drafting that he compulsively had felt the need to do himself.

Can you work effectively if you're too fatigued from excessive hours? Probably not. Maybe a better solution would be to quit early, take the afternoon and evening off, and come back the next day refreshed and physically able to work twice as hard. Get more done by doing nothing. I think you'll find that if you arrange things so that you find time to relax and do nothing, you'll get more done and have more fun doing it.

One client, an aerospace engineer, didn't know how to do nothing. Every minute of his leisure time was scheduled with intense activity. He had an outdoor activity scheduled in which he switched from skiing and ice hockey to camping and tennis. His girlfriend kept up with him in these activities, although she would have preferred just to sit by the fire and relax once in a while. Like too many people, he felt the need to be doing something all the time. Doing nothing seemed a waste of time. His relaxing by the fire consisted of playing chess, reading, or playing bridge. Even his lovemaking was scheduled.

For an experiment, I asked him to waste time for just five minutes during one of our sessions together. What he ended up doing in those five minutes was relaxing, sitting quietly, and daydreaming. When he was finally able to admit that emotional reasons caused him to reject relaxing as a waste of time, he began to look more critically at that assumption. Once he accepted the fact that relaxing was a good use of time, he became less compulsive about being busy and started enjoying each activity more. Previously, he had been so busy doing that he had no time to have fun at anything. He began to do less and have more fun.

CHANGE YOUR SITUATION BY MAXIMIZING YOUR TIME

Sometimes the only way to get more leisure time is to reduce the demands of the job. If you attempt to get more relaxation and don't succeed, you may have to make some basic changes in your work situation.

A credit manager for a men's clothing store struggled with overtime for years. He never could get his boss to let him have an assistant for the details. Finally, after three years suffering, he decided it was hopeless and found a job with another firm where he didn't have to work 80 hours a week and he had more time to spend with his family. On the other hand, the chief accountant in the same firm solved the same overload problem by deciding to do as much as he could and not worry about what didn't get done. His solution of doing things in order of their importance, but only working a regular workweek was more successful. When the boss saw that the work wasn't getting done, he let the chief accountant hire more help. [In the following sections, Lakein showcases some ways you can use time to your advantage.]

Make the Most of Your Transition Time

I have suggested that you need to balance work and play. You might say to me, "I don't have time for everything." Well, I say let's see if we can find you some time. More specifically, let's see if you can find some time that you have previously overlooked.

One kind of time that's often overlooked is what I call transition time. This kind of time starts when you awaken in the morning and ends when you commute to work. For most people it amounts to perhaps 40 minutes a day. One man I know has reduced it though to only 15 minutes. He uses the time only to do essentials—eat breakfast, shave, dress—and he does these as quickly as possible.

There may be an advantage in extending, rather than reducing this transition time, though. If your day is broken into many parts, transition time offers you perhaps the only block of time you'll have alone and undisturbed.

Why not reflect on the best use of your time during the coming day and consider those time management techniques that will help you get things done. There are other ways to enrich transition time, too. For example, one politician was reported to have listened to Shakespeare plays while shaving. One creative manager, realizing that he got some of his best ideas in the morning, has come to expect them and catches them for further development while they and he are still fresh.

Use Commuting and Lunch Time Wisely

If you're a professional person, how about working at home twice a week and skipping that 45-minute commute on the expressway? If you drive to work, true, you're limited in the use you can make of the time you spend while sitting in traffic jams, and safety does come first, but you can listen to the news on the radio, practice your new vocabulary exercise, and as more and more cassette tapes [today, podcasts] on educational subjects are becoming available, you might learn a foreign language, listen to a business report, or take a memory course. Commuting time offers a chance to preview and plan your day, though you should crystalize that plan on paper as soon as you sit down at your desk.

What is the true price of lunch? In some selling jobs, of course, the customer is crucial, and in such a situation a working lunch may be beneficial, but by and large a full-scale lunch is a fantastic waste of time. For most people lunch just adds calories and expenses they can well do without. Many doctors today are dead set against three square meals a day and many first-rate MD diet specialists either skip lunch altogether or have some cottage cheese and that's it. If you take an early or late lunch, the normal lunchtime offers a good opportunity to get things done while the phones are quiet and others are away. On the other hand, if you have a hectic, busy day, a lunch break may provide the only breathing time for you. In that event, if you cut back on your lunchtime, you might decrease your effectiveness the rest of the day. Maybe this is a good time for you to take a walk or swim at the Y.

For example, a general merchandising manager, recently promoted, no longer took a regular lunch hour off. He felt that since his job involved more responsibility, he should be available all the time. And so he just grabbed a quick sandwich on the run. After several weeks of this, he found himself irritable in the afternoon, snapping at his colleagues, and having difficulty concentrating on important matters. I convinced him that he needed a sit-down lunch to restore energy and calm.

How to Use Waiting Time

If you have to wait for the subway, bus, or your carpool or in the prospect's office, you can use those patches of time profitably, too. You might read the paper. But suppose you've had a lifelong goal of reading the classics. Most of them are available now in paperback [or as ebooks and audiobooks]. You may not always feel like reading Don Quixote as you wait for the bus at the corner of Main and Pine, but isn't it nice to have the option? If you're a salesman, you can use waiting time to write up the last order, dictate a follow-up letter, or better prepare yourself for the coming sales talk.

Make Your Sleep Work for You

If you like, you can put some sleep time to work once you realize that most bodily functions continue while you are asleep. As your dreams show, your subconscious works even while you're sleeping. Why not deliberately put it to work on your tough problems? Here's how: Pose a question to your subconscious just before you fall asleep. Select one that requires hours of thought. After all, your subconscious will have four to eight hours to work on it. Now don't waste time thinking about it consciously, but do expect a meaningful answer when you awaken. Many who have tried this method have found it very successful. But if it only keeps you awake, by all means forget it.

How to Repeal Parkinson's Law

I feel that so long as people do the job they're hired and required to do, they shouldn't have to look busy every minute of the time. I've always tried to give the people that work for me a real incentive to make good use of their time by allowing them to do reading, writing, or whatever else they want after they finish my work. I've even sent them home early with full pay when there was nothing else to be done.

The policy of making people sit at their desks even if they have nothing to do breeds bad time habits and accounts for a certain amount of psychological aggravation. "It isn't surprising that work expands to fill the time allotted for its completion," as C. Northcote Parkinson has stated, "since all too often there are no alternatives available." I propose that it's time to repeal Parkinson's Law by allowing people to reap the benefits of getting done early and letting them do their personal things.

In limitless jobs, where there are truly an endless number of things that could be done, such as creating advertising copy, researching, selling, removing every speck of dust from the house, Parkinson's Law theoretically doesn't apply; there is always enough work. In practice, certain tasks tend to be done on a particular day, and these are the ones that are stretched out. You really can't push people to be creative by the clock. And beyond a certain point, simply putting in the hours is not necessarily the best way to get creative work done, as the architect I mentioned earlier clearly demonstrates.

Do More by Doing Less

In all planning, you make a list and you set priorities. It is extremely important to list and set priorities. However, all the items on the list are not of equal value. Once you've made a list, set priorities based on what is important to you now. Use the ABC priority system. Write a capital letter A to the left of those items on the list that have a high value; a B for those with medium value; and a C for those with low value. To a certain extent, you'll have to guess but that's OK; it's still useful. Once you've done that, you're ready to look for tasks that are better left undone.

How often have you resorted to poking through routine work to get a feeling of satisfaction because you're doing the processing efficiently, while you let more important activities go because you want to avoid the feeling of doing them inefficiently.

For example, neatening the desk. You would be unlikely to label this as an A activity, unless it's become a disaster area. But because it's such an easy thing to do and the results show immediately, you might very well spend an extra few minutes, unnecessarily, neatening your desk, when perhaps the thing to do is to get away from your desk and go on and see what you can do with a personnel problem that needs solving down in Department 73.

Why do people have this strong tendency to get bogged down with Cs? One reason is that many activities of top value cannot, by their very nature, be performed well. Part of their value may be that they've never been done before. Examples include setting up a committee to consider manufacturing a new, highly competitive product; diapering a baby for the first time; learning Chinese; switching to organic cooking; or finding something else to do with your evenings besides watching television.

Now there is a certain luxurious feeling that comes from doing whatever you want without regard to priority or time involved. Since you know you're not doing As, you can waste time and gain the feeling of doing something well or starting something easy and finishing it, crossing an item off your list and moving the paper from your inbox to your outbox. But don't kid yourself; it's because you're doing all these Cs, not because you haven't any time, that you don't get to do your As.

Use the 80/20 Rule

When I deal with people who claim they're overwhelmed, one of the best ways I can help them is to have them become more comfortable with not doing Cs. But people are often hesitant to let go of Cs. Therefore, I suggest to you the 80/20 Rule, which says if all items are arranged in order of value, 80 percent of the value would come from only the top 20 percent of the items, while the remaining 20 percent of the value would come from the remaining 80 percent of the items. Sometimes it's a little more, sometimes a little less, but the vast majority of the time I think you'll find the 80/20 Rule is correct.

What this suggests is that in a list of ten items, doing two of them will yield you 80 percent of the value. Find these two, label them A and get them done. Leave most of the other eight undone because the value you'll get from them will be much less than that of the two highest value items. Instead, use your time to find more top priority A items and give them additional time.

A real estate salesman came to me for advice about increasing his sales and profits. We looked over his card file of his properties for sale and his prospect list and discovered that unquestionably, 80 percent of his sales were coming from 20 percent or less of his customers. The 80 percent of his time that was going into low-dollar properties contributed little to his cause. In fact, they wore him out. Being low priced, he had to show them more often, and this took time away from the more expensive and profitable properties. By the end of our talk, the salesman realized that his time was best spent with the cream of the crop. The real payoff for his selectivity came by tripling his earnings in the ensuing 12 months.

When Not to Do Cs

One of the best ways to find time for your As is by reducing the number of Cs that you feel compelled to spend time on. The main question with the Cs is, can I not do this C? Think of the great feeling of satisfaction of drawing a line through a C item on your to-do list, without ever having to go through the effort of doing it. Rather than think I have to do this C, get into the habit of thinking maybe I don't have to do this C.

Let's say your to-do list contains get the car washed. You have given this C priority but are tempted to have a half-hour out and get it washed anyway, just to get it off your mind and off the list. It's much easier to get it off your list and forget about it, by deciding it doesn't need to be done at all. This will give you an extra half-hour of selling time a day and that's high-priority time.

In the ABC priority system, there's something called a Z. A Z is something that doesn't have to get done at all. And many Cs can be turned into what I call CZ's. CZ's are Cs that can be deferred indefinitely without harm. Definite CZ's include rearranging a pile of magazines, mopping the kitchen floor just before the children come home on a rainy day, checking for the morning mail when your secretary always brings it in immediately upon arrival. Some Cs need to be deliberately deferred, to test whether they can become CZ's. Let them age for a while and see if they die a natural death.

Give the ABCs Their Place

Rather than let the high-quality As get buried by the much larger quantity of Cs, try reserving a special place on top of your desk for the A items. Create a special C drawer, where the unimportant items can get dumped safely out of the way. If you already have a C drawer, get yourself a bigger one or a whole cabinet for the Cs. Now as a start, try physically separating your paperwork into small A piles and B piles and a much larger C pile. Resort the B pile into either the A or C group and then put the As in the A place and the Cs in the C drawer.

Sometimes it pays to slow down. What can you do when you have no doubt that you should do the unpleasant A tasks, yet are strongly inclined to run away from it and turn to something else? First, you must recognize clearly when you have reached such a decision time and that you're at the point now of choosing whether to do your A-1 priority now or to avoid it. Once you recognize this decision time, you'll want to take control of the decision-making process. The way to do this is to slow down the final decision. A quick decision to put the unpleasant A-1 out of sight and mind gives you little chance to curb your tendency to procrastinate. Take enough time to consider the situation carefully. Give yourself every opportunity not to ditch the A-1 for some activity of lesser value. Slow down the process so that you have the time to make a conscious and deliberate, favorable choice.

WHEN PERFECTIONISM HELPS AND WHEN IT DOESN'T

Perfectionism is worth approaching when 80 percent of the value comes from the last 20 percent of the effort. For example, the construction of a dam, bringing home the family's favorite groceries, unstopping a plugged-up sink, remembering your wedding anniversary every year. Perfectionism is a waste of time on such labors as rewriting your address book every two months, when there are not many changes or rechecking a low-priority letter for typing errors, when it's already been checked by the typist.

Once you get immersed in such activities, they seem to acquire a momentum of their own. You may then be carried along without control, drifting aimlessly and helplessly with the tide. One way to combat this drift is to set your self-control points for reviewing your progress. Check every 15 minutes or half-hour or go on until 3:30 and then review. One way to remember to do this is to use a timer. If you're not benefiting from continued efforts, stop and change and do something else.

Do you suspect diminishing returns? Are you being needlessly perfectionistic? If you're not sure whether it's worth finishing something or worth continuing, I suggest that you stop. If you don't come back to it, then, in fact, you were done.

PROCRASTINATE POSITIVELY

Perhaps you have been trying to get started on a project, but find yourself continually procrastinating. OK. If you have to procrastinate, I'm going to show you how to do it positively. Sit in the chair and do nothing. That's right, nothing. Don't read a book. Don't shuffle papers. Don't watch TV, just sit completely still. If you sit doing nothing for 15 or 20 minutes, now don't cheat, you must do absolutely nothing, you should become very uneasy. That A-1 priority is staring you right in the face and you're doing nothing. Precious minutes that you could use to accomplish a lifetime goal are slipping by and you're sitting in a chair doing nothing.

Whenever I find myself procrastinating, this is the technique I use. Believe me, after ten minutes at the most, I'm off and running on my A-1. What is you're A-1? What is the best use of your time today? Decide, don't procrastinate, and do it now.

⚜ ENTREPRENEUR ACTION ITEM
Making Time Is Your Most Important Business Resource

It's no secret that proper time management is a crucial element of success regardless of who you are or what you do. Nonetheless, far too few business professionals appreciate time as one of the most important resources around, and precious little is being done in the average workplace to make better use of everyone's most limited asset.

Despite the heavy focus on profitability or the strength of your human capital, managing your time properly is by far the most important element of success in today's market. And yet you're likely wasting it. Here are some tactics to make better use of your working hours.

You Need a Personalized Approach

Most people are familiar with the fact that time management is important, yet precious few understand that you need a personalized approach to seriously achieve any extra efficiency in your day. This is because everyone's schedule is unique. No one else understands the importance of your time during particular periods of your schedule. But to appreciate that yourself it's important you start with an audit of your daily habits to see where you're wasting the most time.

A number of digital apps will show you where you're wasting your time and how to make better use of it. Installing a fancy app on your smartphone or computer will likely help you watch your minutes more closely, and it may even result in some extra productivity, but you need to understand that you're the one in control of your time, not some machine. Successful time management is all about self-control and the ability to honestly assess your own situation to determine when you're dithering vs. when you're making the right decisions.

Only after you've thoroughly and honestly reviewed your daily schedule to see where you're wasting time can you begin to make meaningful life adjustments. Smart time management tips for small-business owners often emphasize a consistent theme—brutal honesty when assessing something's importance is a crucial part of time management.

It's helpful to break down your daily tasks and responsibilities into categories that are ranked by matter of importance. You may discover that you're wasting untold minutes on insignificant duties that can be dedicated elsewhere. Furthermore, categorizing your daily responsibilities in terms of their importance helps you focus on the most urgent and pressing of issues first.

Prioritizing Is the Key to Success

Most time management philosophies revolve around proper prioritization; after all, if you can't understand what needs to be done immediately vs. what can be delayed, you'll always be misapplying your time. Urgent matters that must be dealt with can be brushed under the rug when no one is keeping track of forthcoming deadlines. So, consider maintaining a companywide list of your most pressing business decisions.

A businesswide commitment to deadlines is vitally important; company executives who fail to meet important commitments cannot be let off the hook. Rank-and-file workers who see such behavior will quickly learn that they don't have to deal with urgent matters themselves when the boss doesn't, either.

Make sure everyone in a leadership position understands how to prioritize properly. Employees who are struggling to climb the corporate ladder can be frustrated by managers who don't know how to prioritize their work, so workers should study how to prioritize if their leaders don't know how to.

Company leaders should always be prepared to step in and help employees prioritize when they're struggling with a huge workload. Managers can only be effective when they meddle for the better. But make sure you're not over-analyzing the schedules of each of your workers and micromanaging their every move.

Personalization is imperative to the success of time management. It's important to understand that not everyone prioritizes work-related goals the same. Different workers may employ different time management philosophies. It's crucial to understand what unique approach you need to embrace. Learn how to take a personal approach to keeping close track of your minutes, and you'll be achieving more in no time.

Don't Let Time Management Become a Stressor

Despite how important it is to closely manage your time, it's also true that time management can become a serious stressor if you're not doing it properly. Far too many workers drive themselves to the brink of insanity by keeping a close track of each second as it passes, when in reality all you need to do is have an understandable schedule and a realistic list of priorities. For instance, effective time management that reaches into your personal life shouldn't dictate your free time too much. Closely choreographing your blissful moments of relaxation is just another way of overworking yourself outside the office.

The important takeaway here is that time management is a vital part of success in the modern business world, yet can't be trusted to entirely dictate your life. You always need to leave yourself an unscheduled block of free time that can be used to do whatever you want—maybe it's catching up on work, a favorite TV show, or the list of household chores you've been ignoring for too long. Whatever it is, having some time to "take care of the little things" in your life and forget about the hectic world of your workplace is an important part of staying productive when you're in the office. Time is the most important resource in business precisely because it determines everything else. If you're not carefully balancing your vacation time with your work time, you'll soon find both have been frivolously wasted.

A major part of refusing to let time management become a stressor in your life is learning to focus on the business tasks that are important, rather than just those that are urgent. Meeting important forthcoming deadlines is important, and you should never deliberately ignore a timeline you'd put together in the past. But part of being an expert at time management is understanding that you need to retain a certain degree of flexibility to react to important issues as they arise.

Focus on What's Important

Perhaps the most vital lesson you can learn when it comes to managing your time wisely is that not everything that is urgent is important and vice versa. Sometimes you'll need to take care of an issue immediately but will find it to be of trivial importance. Elsewhere you'll encounter decisions of chief importance to your company that can technically be put off for days, weeks, or even months. Learning to properly categorize your duties and incoming projects so you're more aware of what's important vs. what's urgent is the final step of becoming a time management guru.

Read up on how to schedule important tasks vs. urgent ones, and you'll quickly see that the common elements of flexibility and prioritization turn up anywhere that time management is mentioned. If you refuse to allow anxiety to take hold of you and instead focus on the most pressing issues, you'll soon discover time management is much easier than you imagined. The largest corporations and the smallest mom-and-pop shops alike must make proper use of their time if they want to succeed—and you're no different. Pay close attention to how you're spending your precious time and take some extra steps to more cautiously chart out your days, and your business will soon be thriving.

CHAPTER ELEVEN

Power Over Problems

Dr. Norman Vincent Peale

D r. Norman Vincent Peale was a minister who spent more than 50 years at the Marble Collegiate Church in New York City until his death in 1993 at age 95. Dr. Peale was also a bestselling author, whose themes radiated around the power of positive thinking.

One of Peale's books, T*he Power of Positive Thinking*, was first published in 1960 and is still popular today. It has sold over 7 million copies, and has been published in 15 languages. In this essay, Peale addresses the proverbial elephant in the room— your problems. From big ones to small ones, problems can take over your entire existence until you can't focus on anything BUT them. But to disarm the power of the problem, Peale suggests that you put them in context and remind yourself that you—not your problems—have more power in the situation.

◆ ◆ ◆

START BY CONNECTING WITH OTHERS

I was in Sydney, Australia, speaking to this big convention of Rotarians, and I was the last speaker on the last day of a four-day convention. I spoke from 11:00 to 12:00 in the closing morning [session]. Ahead of me, from 10:00 to 11:00, was a man who was said to be the greatest economist in Australia. And he was pretty dull, really. He was using dull material, and he didn't lighten it up all that much. But he had a technique for holding the audience, which I thought was good. He'd give about 14 minutes of dull material and then he would put in a terrific story. Now none of these stories had any relevance at all to the subject matter, but the audience listened intently through the dull material, until his terrific story would come up.

And one of the stories he told was this one: He said that a professor of psychology went before his class one morning and he looked the boys over and he said, "Gentlemen, Elizabeth II is queen of Great Britain, Jimmy Carter is president of the United States, Hirohito is emperor of Japan. How old am I?" A dead silence fell until a boy in the rear of the room put up his hand and he said, "Professor, you are 44." The professor was astounded. He said, "I am 44, but by what process of logical deduction did you arrive at the fact that I am 44 years of age?" The boy said, "Well, you see, sir, it wasn't all that hard. I have a brother who is in the state insane asylum. He is 22, and you are twice as crazy as he is."

So maybe that's the way it is. But anyway, I want to tell you that you and I are a part of a very historic occasion. I've been going all up and down the country for a good many years, speaking to sales rallies and motivational meetings, and in all that time, and I've spoken I think to some of the largest, this is by all odds the greatest motivational meeting ever put on in the United States of America. And it is due to this gentleman who comes up here and interrupts me periodically, my old and dear friend, W. Clement Stone, and to the president of *Success Unlimited Magazine*, Dwight Chapin, and his associate, Ron Walker.

Only the other day, I read one of the greatest human-interest stories that I have ever seen in all my reading experience. It is the story of the indomitable victory of a human being. It's the story of the fight to survive and to make a contribution against cancer by the senator from this state, Hubert Humphrey. And I suggest that somehow you get hold of that magazine and read that story and keep it in your files when adversity may come to you.

GROWING POSITIVELY THROUGH PROBLEMS

I would like to say to you, from a good long experience, that one minute of time can change our lives from failure to success, from unhappiness to happiness, from sickness to health, whatever the need may be.

One night about three years ago, I was speaking to some three or four thousand sales personnel in a big hall in Cleveland, Ohio. On the way down to the meeting, my taxi cab stopped for a red light. It was a cold, blustery, winter night with a high wind. Across the street from my taxi cab was a gasoline station, and over it was stretched a huge banner advertising some kind of motor oil. And the legend on the banner was this: "A clean engine always delivers power." And I thought to myself *that will be my text for the meeting tonight.*

So I went down there and I drew a connection between a motor engine and that infinitely greater engine known as the human mind and pointed out to the people present that if the human mind is filled with negativisms, with inferior feelings, with inadequate attitudes, with self-doubt, with hate, with resentment, and every other evil thing, how in the world can you expect that the potential power can get through such a mind? And I said, "I don't know who is sitting out here in front of me, but if this description corresponds to you, I'll tell you what you do, sitting right there in that seat. Have a talk with yourself. Be honest with yourself."

I had no sooner got back stage until a big, hulking fellow about 6' 2" came rushing back. He threw his arms around me. He pounded me on the back, and he said, "Boy, do I like you."

"Well," I said, "I like you, but let's not be so vociferous about it." I said, "How come you're so enthusiastic?"

He said, "When you gave that description about an unclean mental motor, you were talking exactly about me. I have been a failure as a husband, as a father, and as a salesman. But I did what you said, right out there in this meeting this afternoon. And I want to tell you something," and he looked at me with a look of wonder on his face. He said, "I have been set free from my fears, from my inferiority, and from my self-doubt, and watch me from now on."

And I have been watching him. He has become a very highly successful, constructive individual. Now one thing is sure. Nobody needs to go through life remaining the way he is or she is, if you shouldn't be that way or if you don't want to be that way. So now here's the thing, the thing that the positive thinker excels in. The positive thinker gets positive results because he or she, the positive thinker, is not afraid of nor baffled by that thing known as a problem.

Now I realize that whenever you mention the word *problem*, the assumption is that you're dealing with something, which in its very nature is inherently bad and ought to be gotten rid of. But nothing could be further from the truth; a problem is and certainly can be inherently good. Every problem contains the seeds of its own solution. And it's out of the problem that the positive thinker grows strong.

⏣ ENTREPRENEUR TIP

Do you only see problems? Maybe it's time to reframe how you think about life's challenges. Start with work, a place where it's probably not hard to identify a few problems. Instead of thinking of those problems as hurdles to success, think of them as opportunities for change. Try this: each day, write down one or two problems you might be facing. Then, jot down two to three ways you can turn those into positive outcomes.

PROBLEMS ARE PART OF LIFE

Yet wherever I go, it seems that people don't like problems. Well, I don't like them too much myself. But they say to me, in effect at least, wouldn't life be simply wonderful if either we had fewer problems or easier problems or better still, no problems whatsoever. Now that's what they say to me.

Would you really and would I really be better off if we had fewer problems or easier problems or no problems at all? Let me answer that question by telling you of an incident. I was walking down 5th Avenue not so long ago, when I saw approaching me a friend of mine by the name of George. It was evident from George's melancholy and disconsonant demeanor that he wasn't what you might say filled to overflowing with the ecstasy and exuberance of human existence, which is a high-class way of saying that George was dragging bottom. He was really low.

Well, this excited my natural curiosity, so I asked him, "How are you, George?" Now, when you get right down to it, that's nothing but a routine inquiry, but it represented an enormous mistake on my part. George spent 15 minutes enlightening me meticulously on how badly he felt. And the more he talked, the worse I felt. So finally, I said to him, "Well, George, what seems to be agitating you; what's got you so upset?" This really set him off.

"Oh," he said, "it's these problems, problems, nothing but problems. I am fed up with problems." And he got so exercised about the matter that he quite forgot who he was talking to and he began to castigate these problems vitriolically, using in the process thereof, I'm sorry to say, a great many theological terms, though he didn't put them together in a theological manner. But I knew what he meant, for he had what the super erudite call a power to communicate.

And I said, "George, I get the idea you're fed up with your problems."

He said, "Norman, you will be my friend for life, if you tell me how to get rid of my problems."

I said, "Alright, I'll try that." But I said, "George, let's get it straight. How many problems do you want to get rid of? Would you like to get rid of a few of them or maybe the most difficult of them?" And I said, "You're not going to stand here on the street this afternoon, are you, and tell me that you want to get rid of all of your problems?"

He says, "The latter is the case. I have had it."

"Oh," I said, "I think I can help you." I said, "George, the other day I was up in the northern part of New York City, in the Bronx, on professional business, if I may thus describe it. And I was in an area up there where the head man told me that by actual count, there were 150,000 people and not a single one of them had a problem."

The first enthusiasm I'd seen in George manifested itself as he says with considerable eagerness, "Boy, that's for me, lead me to this place."

I said, "OK, you asked for it; it's Woodlawn Cemetery in the Bronx." And this is a fact: Nobody in Woodlawn has a problem. They couldn't care less what you and I will hear on television today. They have no problems at all, but they are dead. It follows, therefore, in logical sequence that problems constitute a sign of life.

Indeed, I would go so far as to say that the more problems you have, the more alive you are. An individual who has, let's say, ten good old, tough problems is twice as alive as the poor, miserable, apathetic character who only has five problems. And if you have no problems at all, I warn you, you're on the way out and you don't know it. And what you better do is to head for home and go to your room and shut the door and get down on your knees and pray to the Lord and say to the Lord, *Lord, look, please, what's the matter, don't you trust me anymore, give me some problems.*

IT'S ALL ABOUT ATTITUDE

I don't really believe anybody can be mentally healthy who doesn't take some such attitude as that about a problem. If you want to know whether or not you're mentally unhealthy, you might ask what your reaction is when a tough problem comes along. Do you say, "Why do I get put on like this? I can't handle it. I haven't got what it takes." Then you can pretty well think maybe you're not very healthy-minded. But if on the other hand, you look at the problem and you say, "I can handle any old problem that ever comes up to me in this life."

I would certainly like to hope that you, looking up in the clear, blue heavens would say to yourself, "I believe in myself." And then the next thing is to have a creative attitude, because nobody will ever attain anything other than the attitude that you have. If you have an attitude of defeat, you will suffer defeat. If you have an attitude of achievement, you will experience achievement.

Once I was speaking to the Ohio State Newspaper Association. And I sat all evening beside a wonderful man. I am a great sports fan. I read the sport pages of the newspapers every day before I read the front pages, because when you read the sport pages, you can stand the front pages.

Well, at any rate, this man I was sitting next to was named Jesse Owens, who has been said by some sport writers to be the most supreme athlete ever developed in the United States. Well, I said to him, "Mr. Owens, I would like for you to tell me how you became what you are."

Well, he was modest, and he disclaimed it, but he said, "I'll tell you how I did what I did." He said, "I was born in Cleveland of a family that was materially poor, but spiritually rich; which, if you ask me, is quite a combination." He said, "I was a slender, little, slim, skinny, scrawny kid. I was not very strong, and I didn't know what I wanted to do with my life." But one day, he said, they had an assembly in the school of about a thousand kids. And the speaker on that occasion was a man named Charlie Paddock, who in his time was hailed by sports writers as the fastest human being alive. But now Mr. Paddock had become older, and he was going around speaking to audiences of youth. So, he came out there that day in front of this great crowd and he looked them all over. And he said to them, "Do you know who you are? Well, I'm going to tell you who you are. You can do or be anything you want to be, if you know what it is that you want to be, and if you have the attitude that you can do it, and if you put the image of your goal in your mind, and if you give it all you've got."

Well, little Jesse Owens was sitting down on a front seat. He tells me that immediately he knew exactly what he wanted to be, what he was going to be. He saw the image of it in his mind, right up there in his conscious mind, and he could hardly wait until Paddock finished speaking. And he rushed up and grabbed him by the hands, and he said he could feel an electric impulse pass through his entire body. And then he ran into the coach and he said, "Coach, I know what I want to do. I know what I'm going to be. I've got a dream. I'm going to be the next Charlie Paddock. I'm going to be the fastest human being alive. I've got a dream."

Well, the coach was a wise, old man and put his arms around this little boy, a slender, little shriveled up kid. And he said to him, "That's right, Jesse, have a dream." You'll never go any higher than you can dream, and you're through when you lose your dreams. So, have a dream. But said he, in order to reach your dreams, you've got to build a ladder through your dream. And the first rung of that ladder, he said, this ladder to your dreams, is determination. And the second rung on the ladder to your dreams is dedication. And the third rung on the ladder to your dreams is discipline. And the fourth rung is a creative, positive attitude. You see yourself as achieving your goal. You put the goal into the conscious mind and hold it there as an image, until, by a process of osmosis, it sinks into the subconscious and thereby becomes a part of you.

There is a deep tendency for the human being to become precisely like that which he imagines himself as being. That is to say, you hold the image of what you intend to be and do in your mind and never let it go. You have the attitude that you can. You have to think you can.

Well, now a lot of those kids went out of that meeting that day and they forgot all about this ladder to your dreams and everything. But there came a day in Berlin when Jesse Owens got a whole handful of gold medals. He ran the 100-meter faster than any human being in history. Likewise, he ran the 200-meter at a speed that nobody had ever achieved. His broad-jump record stood for 25 years. And when they established the American Hall of Athletic Fame, whose name was inscribed at the top? None other than the little, skinny kid from Cleveland, Jesse Owens, who had the attitude.

⬥ ENTREPRENEUR TIP

Check your attitude! Cultivating a positive attitude toward change can help you better tackle the tasks necessary to see the results of your hard work. Set some achievable, measurable goals for yourself, then set your attitude toward success. Approaching those tasks with the attitude that you can do it will help you actually DO it. So whether it's improving your exercise habits or working toward being more assertive in meetings, believe you can . . . and you WILL.

THINK POSITIVELY

Now I know you get discouraged at times; you get frustrated. You get so you don't believe in yourself. Sometimes you even come to the point almost where you're willing to chuck it all and try something else, the heck with it, and so forth. And you might walk up to me and say, "Let me tell you the problem I've got." Now you don't need to do that, because I know what human problems are. And let me tell you this, there is no problem, no difficulty so tough that you—and I mean this with all my heart—that you can't handle it, if you believe in yourself and if you believe that you can.

So, the next thing that the positive thinker has to do is simply to think positively. Now broadly speaking, there are two ways in which you can think. Either you can think negatively or you can think positively. Now the negative thinker does a very dangerous thing. He constantly pumps out into the world around him negative thoughts, and he activates the world around him negatively.

There is a law known as the law of attraction. Light attracts light. Birds of a feather flock together. Thoughts of a kind have a natural affinity. So if you constantly send out negative thoughts, in the very nature of the case, you draw negative results back to yourself. Like a man I met on the airplane the other day; I was flying from LaGuardia to O'Hare. And there was a guy, and I sat down next to him. He had a sour look on his face. I said to him, "How are you?"

He said, "So what." He said to me, "Well, I've got to ask how you are?"

I said, "Well, I'm fine."

"Oh," he said, "don't talk that way, it makes me feel worse."

And I thought *I'm going to have a very inspiring conversation*, but finally he clammed up. So I picked up the paper and began to read it, and suddenly, I was interrupted by this man saying to me, without any introduction whatsoever, "Why does everything go wrong with me?" Well, now how in the world did I know? I had never even seen him up until that minute.

"Well," I said, "I'll tell you, my friend, why don't you talk to me for 15 minutes so that I can get the color of your mind and maybe then I can give you a wise judgment on why everything goes wrong with you?" And he began to talk, not for 15 minutes, but for 40 minutes, and I never in all my life heard such a mass of negativism, inferiority, inadequacy, hate, and every old other kind of thing as poured out of this fellow's mind.

And I was about to give him a prescription to help him, when all of a sudden, he said, "Hold it, hold it." Well, I wasn't holding anything. I wasn't saying anything. He said, "Hold it. I know why everything goes wrong with me." He said, "I just saw it as clear as can be. I know why everything goes wrong with me." I asked why. He said, "Because I am wrong myself."

I said, "Brother, you have had what is known in the trade as an *insight*."

It is a fact that in thinking never produces right results. It's impossible. Only right thinking produces right results. Well, now the positive thinkers on the other hand, they are a great breed of human being. They are filled with hope, expectation, and optimism. They are a believer, and a believer always sweeps everything before themselves. And a positive thinker pumps out positive thoughts and attitudes into the world, and on the basis of the same law of attraction, draws back positive results.

Now if you're not a positive thinker, it's perfectly possible to become one by reading positive literature, by associating with positive people, by practicing the techniques of belief and faith. You can do anything with yourself that you want to do, provided you want to do it badly enough. And when you become a positive thinker, you become a clear thinker and you become a person who knows that they can handle their difficulties.

Like a boy, a friend of mine, he's 16. He is some boy. He is the son of a friend of mine. Last spring when the vacation came along, he went to his father and he said, "Look, Dad, I don't want to sponge on you anymore; I want to get a job of my own and make some money."

The father, after he recovered from his shock, said, "Well, son, that's great, but the job market for boys your age is pretty tough right now. I don't think you can get a job."

The boy said, "Dad, I have learned to be a positive thinker, and I have learned one thing, that where there is a desire, there is out there the satisfaction of that desire. And I have a desire for a job, therefore, there is a job out there that has a desire for me, and all I have to do by positive thought, is bring them together."

The father, despite himself, was impressed. He said, "Let's see you work it."

So the boy got out the newspaper, and he read the want ads, and they found an ad that suited his specifications, and the advertisement said, "Wanted: A boy, 16." That was his age. It read, "Show up at a certain address on 42nd Street tomorrow morning at eight o'clock and be prompt." The boy was down there the next morning, certainly not at 8:15, not even at 8:00. He was down there at 7:45, only to find that there were 20 boys lined up, leading to the secretary of the man doing the hiring, which made him the 21st kid in line. He looked the boys all over and had to admit to himself they were good boys. He said if he were the boss, he would hire any one of them. But he didn't want any one of them hired; he was a competitor out of the American free-enterprise system. This was his competition—this was his problem—how to get from the lowly 21st position over the heads of 20 good boys and get the boss's attention. I said, "What did you do?"

He said, "I thought, and I thought positively," and he said, "I got an idea." And when you do that, you'll always get an idea, inevitably, indubitably. So, he took a piece of paper and he wrote something on it. He folded it up neatly, and he walked over to the secretary of the man doing the hiring. He bowed respectfully to her, and he said, "Miss, it is very important that your boss get this note immediately."

Now she was an old, hardened hand, and had he been an ordinary boy, she would have said, "Forget it, sonny, don't bother me, get back in the 21st position where you belong." But intuitively, she picked up the consciousness that here was an unusual boy and so grudgingly she said, "Show me the note."

He showed her the note, and she smiled. She immediately got up from her place, and she walked into the boss's office, and she put the note down on his desk. He read it and he laughed out loud, for this is what it said, "Dear Sir, I am the 21st kid in line. Don't do anything until you see me."

HARNESS THE POWER OF ENTHUSIASM

So that's it. First of all, you've got to know that you can change. I've got to know that I can change. I'm not satisfied with myself, not at all. I'm working at it, and I keep telling myself I can do better. And I believe I can. So can you.

Then the next thing is, you've got to be a philosopher and a student of this thing known as the problem and to know that a problem is good for you, because it grows you strong.

And then in the next place you develop an attitude that you can, if you think you can, provided you have the goal and hold the image. And then you become a positive, not a negative thinker.

And then there's just one more thing: You've got to be enthusiastic. What did you say when you got up this morning? "It's going to be a great day?" Do you love your job? Now you're probably not going to go back to work until tomorrow. But can you hardly wait to get there?

Then there's enthusiasm! Somebody asked me the other day, as though I knew anything about it, what is the greatest word in the English language? Well, I thought a minute and being a minister, I had to fall back on the Bible, so I said, "It's love, because the Bible says, 'And now abideth faith, hope and love, these three. But the greatest of these is love.'" And that makes faith and hope second and third. So, then what would be number four? Well, my nomination of the words in the English dictionary is the word *enthusiasm*. It sweeps everything before it, overcoming every resistance and difficulty, if you really got it. And it lifts a human being up and makes them really alive.

You see, when a baby is born, it is full of enthusiasm. Did you ever see a negative baby? Well, how do they get to be negative? Because they live with negative people. The best thing you can do for your children is be positive and enthusiastic.

Tomorrow morning when you wake up, throw back the bed covers with a majestic gesture of self-assertion and leap out of bed and say, "I feel wonderful." Then go into your shower and as you take your bath, sing. Sing because it will wash out of the mind the old, tired, dead, listless, negative thoughts of yesterday as you wash your body with soap and water.

Then getting out of that shower, get dressed and feel alive to your fingertips. Go downstairs to the dining room and sit down to breakfast.

Then when you put a good breakfast under your belt, go out into your terrace or your breezeway or whatever you got out there and stand tall, reaching for the sky with the crown of your head and drink in the good old, crisp October air.

Then standing there in the morning air, say, "Do you know who I am? Well, I'm going to tell you, I am an American businessperson. I am an American salesperson. I am an American professional, and I'm going downtown today in this great community of Bloomington and Minneapolis and St. Paul, and I'm going to deal in goods and services all day long; and I'm going to have the time of my life doing it."

Do these things and you'll be a positive thinker who gets positive results, and you'll have the time of your life, all your life.

ENTREPRENEUR ACTION ITEM
Use Six Principles for Overcoming Entrepreneurial Adversity

Problems and adversity can be motivational, as Dr. Peale explained in this chapter. Why? Because, as he said, "it grows you strong." In other words, a life lived without some adversity is going to be a stunted one. Make that adversity work for you. Every entrepreneur knows what it's like to face problems and adversity. It comes with the territory, and includes cash flow challenges, fickle customers, belligerent investors, and unpredictable economic downturns. The best entrepreneurs tackle these one at a time without losing their stride or their passion and many secretly get their highest satisfaction from overcoming an impossible problem.

For example, you probably didn't know that one of the world's richest entrepreneurs, Bill Gates, found that his first venture, Traf-O-Data, failed to make money because he couldn't solve the technical problems quickly enough and selling to municipalities was a nightmare. Instead of making excuses, he credited his later success with Microsoft to the lessons he learned with Traf-O-Data.

Also, most people don't realize that Richard Branson has dyslexia, which made him a poor student, so he faced adversity well before his first startup effort. Yet he was able to use his dynamic and powerful personality to drive him to success. Today, Branson is known for over 400 companies, many technologically advanced, and he is one of the richest people in the United Kingdom.

Adversity can often energize some people, almost to the super-human level, while others are driven to despair. It may start with a strong survivor instinct, rather than reverting to a victim mentality. Beyond this, here is a set of principles we recommend for every founder in the face of adversity.

Maintain a Positive Attitude and Learn from Failure

Thomas Edison called every failure an experiment (now it would be a pivot). He made no excuses for 10,000 light-filament failures. Challenged by his contemporaries, Edison soberly responded: "I have just found 10,000 ways that won't work." He then succeeded.

Build Relationships with Others

An isolated position is hard to defend in the face of adversity. Successful entrepreneurs are not afraid to reach out and ask for help from peers and advisors. They communicate their goals, fears, and challenges without excuses and listen to feedback and guidance.

Surround Yourself with Smarter People

The best entrepreneurs get past the need to control every aspect of their business and make every decision. They solicit people who are strong, have more expertise in a specific area, and trust them to make decisions there. Adversity will melt away.

Prioritize Your Health

In the natural world of survival, unhealthy and unbalanced people most easily succumb to adversity. Smart entrepreneurs always find time for rest, outside physical activities, or even meditation. Working 20 hours a day, seven days a week does not solve all problems.

Accept Adversity as a Norm Rather Than an Exception

Some adversity is inevitable in every business, so it must be treated as any other unknown, rather than a crisis or the end of the world. Many entrepreneurs thrive in adversity and get satisfaction from solving challenges, compared to the relative boredom of business-as-usual.

Practice Resilience By Refocusing on Your Strengths

Researchers have concluded that human beings are born with an innate self-righting ability or resilience, which can be helped or hindered. Obsessing about problems and weaknesses hinders resilience, while identifying and building on individual strengths increases resilience and leads to success.

One of the biggest myths that aspiring entrepreneurs tend to believe is that they can be successful doing only fun things. In reality, experienced leaders and entrepreneurs will tell you that it's how you anticipate and handle the inevitable tough challenges that determine long-term happiness. If you try to avoid any risk and competition, you won't be happy with the outcome.

The entrepreneur lifestyle isn't for those who can't deal with risk and adversity. We can all benefit from the experiences of others. The best entrepreneurs don't succeed by dodging challenges, but because of how they handle them.

A Reader's Guide to *Napoleon Hill's Success Masters*

From advice on habits to meditations on mindfulness, the writers and thinkers featured in *Napoleon Hill's Success Masters* have shared some of the most evergreen advice on success with you. As you've likely noticed, their classic writings on what creates, supports, and sustains success all approach the topic differently. But one narrative thread connects them all in a tapestry that gives you, the reader, a comprehensive road map to success: the thread of personal development. What makes you successful is . . . you. And you are the architect of your own success story.

✦ ✦ ✦

Now that you have had a chance to hear from some of the world's foremost experts on success, you can start to apply those lessons to your own journey. To help you do that, the editors at *Entrepreneur* have designed a reader's guide that will help you revisit the stories, anecdotes, and lessons from these Success Masters and think about them more deeply. The discussion questions below are designed to help you identify what speaks to you most in this book while, at the same time, help you identify what is most important to you about your own success journey. Feel free to use these discussion questions not just once, but often, as you move toward your own goals. Why often? Because everyone's mileage may vary on the journey to success. What's important to you today may be replaced by a new goal, idea, or priority down the road. That's why the lessons here are timeless, and these questions are created to travel with you every step of the way.

DISCUSSION QUESTIONS

What author speaks to you the most at this particular moment in time?

What advice can you apply to your own journey right now? Do you envision your answer changing over time? How about in the next year, or five years?

What Success Master speaks to your own experiences? Why?

If you could identify three key takeaways from each essay, what would they be? How do they apply to your own success journey?

What is your favorite quote or concept in this book? Why?

As you begin to see yourself and your own journey reflected in these essays, think about advice you've gotten over the years. Do any of the suggestions or concepts in this book remind you of success strategies you've heard in your own life? If so, how?

Share some favorite quotes from the book with someone you interact with on your own success journey. How you can you explain those quotes to a mentee or someone who has coached or mentored you?

If you could have a personal chat with any of the authors in this book, what would you ask them?

If you could take any of the essays here and put your own spin on it, what would you change? How would you help apply lessons from your own life to what the Success Masters have already written?

What is something you learned in this book that you didn't already know?

Do any of the essays spark new questions for you about your own success journey? What are they?

What advice in the book is most relatable to you? The least? Why?

What common themes do you see running through the essays?

How do those common themes apply to you?

If you wrote your own essay on success, what would it be about? Would that topic change over time?

Think about your five- and ten-year goals. Where do you want to be? What do you want to be doing? If you could assign your future self an essay to read based on those goals, what would it be? Why?

Resources

The Entrepreneur Action Item sections that accompany each selection are derived from articles and content originally appearing on entrepreneur.com. They include:

"8 Habits of Highly Effective Entrepreneurs" by Sherrie Campbell, https://www.entrepreneur.com/article/327113

"5 Ways to Rewire Your Brain to Be Positive" by Deep Patel, https://www.entrepreneur.com/article/296779

"6 Reasons Why You Need to Mastermind Your Business" by Lain Ehmann, https://www.entrepreneur.com/article/274315

"8 Keys to Coming Off as the Expert in Whatever You Sell" by Marc Wayshak, https://www.entrepreneur.com/article/295703

"What Smart Entrepreneurs Know About Problem Solving" by Dipti Parmar, https://www.entrepreneur.com/article/313089

"15 Ways to Drown Out the Destructive Voices in Your Head" by Lydia Belanger, https://www.entrepreneur.com/article/289160

"How to Live with Purpose and Stay Focused on Long-Term Goals" by Dan Dowling, https://www.entrepreneur.com/article/315502

"The 7 'Senses' of Self-Development" by Sherrie Campbell, https://www.entrepreneur.com/article/331147

"This Is What It Takes to Spark Change in Your Life" by Raul Villacis, https://www.entrepreneur.com/article/325937

"Why Time Is Your Most Important Business Resource" by Chris Porteous, https://www.entrepreneur.com/article/328205

"6 Principles for Overcoming Entrepreneurial Adversity" by Martin Zwilling, https://www.entrepreneur.com/article/275571

About Napoleon Hill

Napoleon Hill was born in 1883 in a one-room cabin on the Pound River in Wise County, Virginia. He began his writing career at age 13 as a "mountain reporter" for small-town newspapers and went on to become America's most beloved motivational author. Hill passed away in November 1970 after a long and successful career writing, teaching, and lecturing about the principles of success.

Dr. Hill's work stands as a monument to individual achievement and is the cornerstone of modern motivation. His book, *Think and Grow Rich*, is the all-time bestseller in the field. Hill established the Napoleon Hill Foundation as a nonprofit educational institution whose mission is to perpetuate his philosophy of leadership, self-motivation, and individual achievement. Learn more about Napoleon Hill at www.naphill.org.

Index